Changing Strategic Direction

Peter Skat-Rørdam

Changing Strategic Direction

Practical Insights into Opportunity Driven Business Development

In association with
Daniel F. Muzyka, INSEAD
and
Ernst & Young Management Consulting

WITHDRAWN
UTSA LIBRARIES

Copenhagen Business School Press
Handelshøjskolens Forlag

Changing Strategic Direction

© Handelshøjskolens Forlag, *Copenhagen Business School Press*, 1999
Printed in Denmark 1999
Set in Plantin and printed by AKA-PRINT, Denmark
Cover designed by Kontrapunkt
Book designed by Jørn Ekstrøm

ISBN 87-16-13430-3

Distribution

Scandinavia:
Munksgaard/DBK, Siljangade 2-8. P.O. Box 1731,
DK-2300 Copenhagen S, Denmark,
phone: + 45 3269 7788, fax: +45 3269 7789

North America:
Copenhagen Business School Press
Books International Inc.
P.O. Box 605
Herndon, VA 20172-0605, USA
phone: + 1 703 661 1500, fax: + 1 703 661 1501
E-mail: intpubmkt@aol.com

Rest of the World:
Marston Book Services, P.O. Box 269,
Abingdon, Oxfordshire, OX14 4YN, UK
phone: +44 (0) 1235 465500, fax: +44 (0) 1235 465555
E-mail Direct Customers: direct.order@marston.co.uk
E-mail Booksellers: trade.order@marston.co.uk

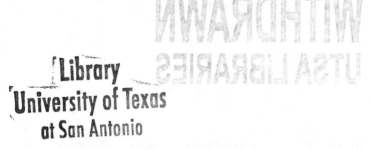

Preface

This book is based on 4 reports written between 1995 and 1996 while I was working at INSEAD, the leading European business school, on leave of absence from Ernst & Young Management Consulting. I was working at INSEAD as an "executive-in-residence". INSEAD occasionally offers practitioners, business managers or consultants the opportunity to gain experience as "executives-in-residence", dealing with issues normally ignored due to busy work-schedules.

The extremely stimulating INSEAD environment offers a unique setting for practitioners to blend personal practical experience with INSEAD know-how.

Interest in the topic of this book began during a strategy consulting engagement with an Ernst & Young client that had been unable to capitalize on business opportunities generated by radically changing markets. The company was maintaining the same strategic course that had served it well for many years. The consultants working on the project discovered that their own strategy consulting tool-box lacked the necessary tools required to facilitate discussion or implementation of change in strategic direction. This spurred my interest in investigating how other companies dealt with changing direction.

It seems fair to say that strategy practitioners and academics have been going through a considerable amount of soul-searching. Strategic planning, almost by definition, is not the answer to finding ways through rapidly changing environments that are difficult to forecast. This book aims to explore the current new wave of strategy thinking, and to look at the experiences of companies that have successfully changed direction and exploited new opportunities. *The book offers a simple and straight forward perspective on what we call the opportunity driven approach to business development.*

This book might not have been completed if Anker Nielsen, former partner of Ernst & Young Management Consulting, and Professor Dan Muzyka of INSEAD, had not from the beginning supported the ideas and the project. For this, I offer my sincere gratitude. My thanks also to those at INSEAD and within the Ernst & Young organization who provided valuable comments, ideas and support.

I would like to emphasize that, regardless of whether the global business climate is good or bad, there will always be business opportunities out there in the market, though the nature of these opportunities and the costs involved in exploiting them may differ.

Enjoy your reading.

Peter Skat-Rørdam

Table of Contents

Part One

Changing Strategic Direction

1.1 Introduction

This book, "Changing Strategic Direction", is the result of a project undertaken in the mid-1990s under the auspices of INSEAD. The project was prompted by the author's experiences in industry, management consultancy and academics, where I learned that classical strategy tools no longer appeared capable of producing the foresight and creative new strategies necessary for success within the radically changing market conditions of the 1990s. Utilizing these tools felt kind of like using a screwdriver to repair a modern engine with on-board computer electronic fuel-injection.

"Changing Strategic Direction" therefore examines the following three topics:

1 The forces that are currently changing competition and markets, and how these have influenced the concept of business strategy;
2 Actions taken in recent years by successful companies to exploit change and/or initiate change in their industries. This includes the way they have shaped their strategies for doing so;
3 The development of a new approach to strategy formulation that is relevant to the challenges that companies are likely to face in the new millennium.

The conclusions related to the above topic no. 3. are based on detailed discussions with five European companies that have successfully changed direction, as well as on the ideas of leading business thinkers and on the author's personal experience.

The annual turnover of the five companies considered in these case studies ranges between USD 25 million and USD 400 million. This does not, however, mean that the report's conclusions apply only to companies within that range. In my view these finding are of equal relevance to smaller companies, as well as to major international concerns.

What is "business strategy"?

There are probably as many definitions of the phrase "business strategy" as there are management theorists, and there is in fact a great deal of soul-searching going on at the moment into the nature of business strategy. For our purposes, however, strategy will be defined in practical terms, simply as the answer to: "Where do we want to go, and how do we get there?".

In other words, the formulation of a business strategy should include decisions on *direction* as much as it does implementation.

Strategy focuses on a company's main building blocks, its business foundation, including:

1 What it offers for sale;
2 Its sources of competitiveness and profits;
3 The way it organizes human resources, systems and technologies in order to deliver 1) and 2).

A company's decisions regarding its business foundation form a pattern that results in a strategic direction. In my experience, this direction is seldom described in its entirety in any strategic business plan. The actual direction often merely *emerges*, based on implementation of an intended strategy direction. Thus the key success factors of a strategy cannot be understood solely by reading a business plan.

Simply stated, the purpose of the strategy discipline is to provide guidelines and frameworks, etc. that will help a company become more successful in both the short and long term by establishing a direction for the business.

The essential element in a strategy is not the detailed planning, rather it is the *thinking* that lies behind these fundamental corporate decisions. In some situations, such as when investors are being sought after, a business plan is important. However, as Ahmar Bhide (1994) said: "...businesses cannot be launched like space shuttles, with every detail of the mission planned in advance".

Strategic thinking is a process that is constantly in the minds of decision-makers and those with influence at all levels in an organization. Strategic thinking and implementation are as much about the short and medium terms as they are about the long term. Today's successful companies change their competitive strategies often.

In a dynamic and continuously changing business environment, organizational flexibility and anticipation are important, but not sufficient in themselves. There has to be thought, a form of logic, that can change, guiding a company's moves in a profitable manner. As with muscle and brain, one is useless without the other.

In this book, the perspective on strategy is that of companies which need to change direction fairly rapidly. In such situations, building an adaptable or learning organization is not a quick solution to the problem. If someone is already sick and serious treatment is needed, perhaps even surgery, it would be futile for a doctor to suggest at that point that a healthier life style would be the best cure.

Cutting costs is often not the right strategy

When there is need for improvement in a company's profitability, two options are typically considered, which are increasing revenue and decreasing costs. In the early 1990s, when economic growth was low in Europe, managements under pressure to produce better results often preferred to reduce costs by downsizing, canceling expenditure programs and re-engineering business processes. This has proven in the past to be a fairly reliable and reasonably quick way to achieve better profits, whereas attempting to increase revenue through things like creative pricing policies, promotional activities and targeting new customers is riskier and longer-term.

But there are two problems with cost-cutting, the first of which is that it often only produces short term results. If the money saved is not quickly reinvested into creating new products and services, or image, etc., the consequences can be stagnating sales and revenue. The second problem with the cost-cutting approach is that it does not take into consideration the need, especially in a turbulent world, for thinking and creativity in relation to products and services in order to maintain, not to mention increase, revenue in both the short and long term.

Strategic thinking and action should be among the principles a company uses to create and capitalize on opportunities in the market.

Part Two

**Forces behind market change and the new
wave of strategic thinking**

2.1 Forces behind competitive and market change

Forces, change and opportunity – an overview

Understanding the catalysts or forces of change that affect a company's business conditions is vital to success. This is different from making five-year market forecasts or describing what the world will look like in the year 2005. The important point in this context is being able to anticipate the forces that will motivate change and create opportunities in the future, rather than merely trying to describe what the future will look like. Whether these forces of change are economic, technological, social or political is not particularly significant. They all feed, or create themselves, industrial and market change.

The forces considered below have been developing for years. They are present today and are unlikely to fade away anytime soon. They are elements that create turbulence and that have an impact on competition. Such forces differ in nature, some developing systematically, while others develop in a disorganized or unpredictable manner. The latter forces are those that pose the greatest challenges.

Turbulence is always with us. The turbulence and forces of change we have been experiencing in the 1990s are not necessarily more powerful or more dramatic than those of the 1960s and 1970s, even though we might see things that way.

In this context, it is important to recognize that change is brought on by more than just events that are external to the industry concerned, such as political or technological developments. Often change is triggered by one or more companies (and essentially the people in them) modifying the rules of the competitive game within a given industry, for instance by changing customer choices.

The consideration of forces in this section of the book is not a scientific overview, but is a starting point for discussion. I have selected the eight important forces shown in the following diagram.

Forces of competitive and market change

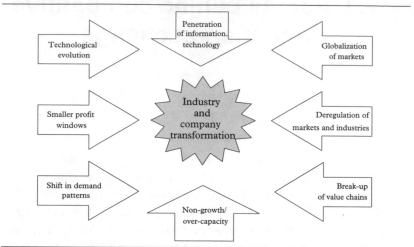

Penetration of information technology (IT)

Futurologists, management philosophers and others frequently speak of the *information revolution*. This is a misleading label for the series of changes we are currently experiencing in this field. Revolution is abrupt by definition, whereas this transformation of communication patterns has been a long, continuous evolutionary process. It arguably began in the mid-1980s with the introduction of the personal computer.

The general message from the experts is that we are in the middle of a transition from an industrial society to an information society, comparable to the transition from an agricultural society to an industrial society in the 19th Century. There are those who predict that the penetration of IT will have the same radical effect on society as printing had at the time of its invention.

The "information revolution" has found its means of expression most clearly in two ways:

- IT devices and services are now embodied in the PC, and various on/off-line systems have become essential elements in daily life;
- Electronically stored information has become an important asset, substituting itself for various physical assets, such as paper money and documents, etc.

As a consequence, the ability to exploit IT is becoming as important for companies as using the telephone.

Borders between industries are being erased

IT is erasing borders between industries, with the IT industry itself being the best example. The core hardware, software, and communication-infrastructure industries are in the process of melting together, taking parts of the consulting industry along with them.

IT companies are also linking up with information and entertainment content providers, including newspapers, television channels and film studios. Links to information-heavy industries, such as the financial services sector, are also starting to occur. The logic behind such alliances is that, in a world where information, entertainment and communication converge, both distribution and content must be controlled in order to achieve economies of scale. Such cross-industry constellations are altering the competitive picture because they control all elements of the value-chain for the end-consumer. They are also pooling their resources in order to undertake the costly projects needed to realize the full potential of new technology.

Even in the watch industry, which used to be dominated by old craft companies in Switzerland, the information technology company, Casio, is a leading player. Many fashion-industry companies are involved as well. Swatch actually defines its watches as fashion accessories.

In other words, boundaries between industries are generally becoming "fuzzy", because business can be gained by borrowing concepts from other industries.

New products, services and industries being created

New developments in IT create new products that are often substitutes for existing products. Electronic communications products are gradually replacing the traditional letter, and national mail services are increasingly in competition with electronic net operators.

Home shopping via interactive television and the Internet has begun, though it is still in its infancy. For example, you can visit a virtual record shop, listen to CDs, order them, pay electronically and have the CDs delivered. The next step will be replacement of the need to physically mail the product by downloading it direct to the buyer's computer.

Such developments have profound implications for business, affecting both the nature of products and services, and the ways in which these are marketed. Advertisers are currently looking for ways to achieve readership of advertisements placed on the Internet comparable to that for newspaper advertisements. The problems are that readers of electronic newspapers are selective and that advertising space (limited by screen size) is small. Readers of traditional newspapers usually leaf through all the pages and thus are exposed to more advertisements.

It is worth pointing out at this juncture that the entry barriers to new players in IT-based industries are very low. The personal computer industry was born in a garage by a company called Apple, and the world's current leading software company, Microsoft, had similar modest beginnings. There are therefore rich opportunities to develop and market new services with "just" a computer and a link to the Internet. New companies providing services related to the Internet and multimedia are flowering all over the world. Quite a number of them are listed on the NASDAQ stock exchange, including Netscape (the Internet browser), Macromedia (multimedia software) and Autodesk (3D software).

There is a battle over standards

Companies with new products and services based on IT are in the process of setting standards and formats, as in any new market. This is especially important in this field, since *connectivity* and *interaction* are basic requirements. Competing for standards is often very costly, and losing such a battle can be fatal.

The information asset is spread

Information stored in many databases around the world can be freely accessed via the Internet, and means have been developed to undertake this task automatically using specialized software. Satellite television is also a medium that spreads information very rapidly, meaning yet another entry barrier has thereby been removed. The major companies which have historically used their financial power to gather and monopolize information no longer have this advantage.

Globalisation of markets

It has become easier to sell products or exploit and leverage business concepts without regard to national boundaries. There are three main reasons why markets have become global:

First: Consumers in the "triad" (North America, Europe and Japan) have developed more homogeneous life styles and demand certain patterns (especially the younger age groups).As a result, products like the Walkman have universal appeal;

Second: This homogeneity makes serving the global market much more financially attractive, particularly now that freer trade makes it difficult to achieve a special position in any single or limited number of markets;

Third: In some industries, e.g. pharmaceuticals, development costs have escalated to a point where world-wide sales is the only way to achieve an adequate return on investment.

Companies tend to think of global markets as being large, but there is also a tendency to create smaller global markets, with an increase in the number of market segments and niches. This is especially true in low-growth sectors like the car industry, which increased to 24 segments from 18 in the private-car market between 1978 and 1985, as reported by Nevens, Summe and Uttal (1990).

Even smaller industries involving medium-sized companies are becoming global. The hearing-aid industry, with a global turnover of USD 1-1.5 billion, is becoming a global industry because the cost of developing new hearing aids is rapidly reducing the number of players to a small number of companies that are able to market their products all over the world. A key element in global sales involving limited volume is to develop a cost-effective distribution system.

Terms like "born global" and "micro-multinational" are used to describe small and medium-sized companies in high-tech industries (e.g. biotechnology, software and electronics), that begin life in an international market.

Both in consumer goods and the business-to-business market, it has become easier to sell a single product all over the world. But marketing still has to respect cultural differences, even between countries in Europe. If you have limited international experience, going global can still be a dangerous game.

Transnational companies

Transnational companies operate, invest and own substantial assets in many countries. They are important drivers of economic activity, knowledge transfer and jobs. A number of such companies – Gillette, McDonald's, IKEA, Toys R Us and Coca Cola, for example – penetrate market after market very successfully. According to a 1994 report from the United Nations, there were at that time 37,000 transnational companies, with a total turnover of USD 5,000 billion. The world's 100 biggest transnationals have a combined turnover of around USD 3,500 billion and control approximately 15-20 % of GNP in the OECD countries.

With today's shorter product life-cycles, many transnational companies try to achieve the maximum pay-off from new products by exercising a single global launch into the market. The chance of big success is higher, but so are the odds for big failure.

Many smaller and medium-sized companies become business partners with these transnational companies. IKEA, for example, has contracts with several smaller Danish furniture manufacturers for production in accordance with IKEA's international specifications. McDonald's relies on local suppliers for many of their burger ingredients.

The global electronics market

Satellite television transmission, the Internet and fax machines are all examples of media that make it easier and less expensive for companies to reach customers on a world-wide basis. Even sales calls can be made electronically, through video conferencing. Use of these media may lower resistance to "smallness", another traditional entry barrier. On the Internet, you cannot really tell whether a company is big or small, as one expert explained.

Doing business in Asia

Asia has had the fastest-growing markets in the world for many years. Though this growth has slackened off in the late 1990s, these markets are still very interesting. "Business Week" reported a couple of years ago that the ASEAN countries, China (including Hong Kong), Korea and Taiwan, will spend USD 1.9 trillion by the year 2000 on transport, power, telecommunications and other infrastructure projects. This figure does not include investment in India, which is forecast to have a population almost as big as China's by 2020.

Many transnationals are important players in these growth markets. A number of companies have found that an effective way to develop business in China is by forming joint ventures with local partners or international companies that are already established there.

But doing business in Asia is not easy. It takes time to learn the myriad of different business cultures, languages and traditions. And even though the potential is enormous, there is lively competition from many companies "going for the gold".

Deregulation of markets and industries

There is currently a world-wide trend for deregulation in telecommunications, air transport, postal services, television and energy, all industries that used to be regulated by government. Deregulation has opened up a wide range of new business opportunities. This has completely changed competitive patterns for infrastructure industries, and also influences industries closely linked to them. The liberalization of transportation, for example, is affecting industries reliant on efficient logistics, like wholesaling and retailing. The deregulation of telecommunications is affecting the media industry.

New business opportunities even exist in the crowded air transport business. New airlines are being established every year in Asia. In the USA, small airlines are filling the gaps major carriers do not handle, acting as feeders for trunk routes.

Barriers and regulation still exist

There are still, however, many barriers for companies wishing to "go international", even within the EU. A Danish company wanting to set up a subsidiary in France needs to exercise considerable patience, especially if it wants a Dane as its local manager. The "single market", allegedly created in 1992, has yet to become a reality.

In some areas, regulation is even increasing:

- Environmental controls are more and more evident;
- The pharmaceutical industry is under price regulation in various countries;
- Biotechnology companies must observe strict regulations relating to genetic manipulation.

Whole markets are also regulated. Some Asian markets, for example, are still under relatively strong government control. A prerequisite for success in these markets is very often a partner with good governmental contacts.

Break-up of company and industry value chains

Companies are dismantling their own value-chains in order to improve their basic financial status. The consequence can sometimes be a complete change in an industry's structure and competitive dynamics.

Breaking up company value chains

Companies have been typically accustomed to organizing themselves with all their main functions – production, administration, development and sales & marketing – in one place, ensuring effective communication and control. Today, however, this centralization of physical location may no longer be necessary. Electronic communication and free trade have made it possible to place these primary functions at the most beneficial locations, anywhere in the world.

Danish companies in the clothing industry would not have survived, and newer firms might never have been established, if they had not used a "global production" concept. Eccolet, a shoe manufacturer, is a good example, as reported by the newsletter "Mandag Morgen" in 1995 (see page 25).

Dismantling the value chain and outsourcing parts of it turn fixed costs into variable costs and increase flexibility. But logistics and control become more complicated.

The break-up of industry value chains

The traditional division between production and distribution is disappearing in certain industries. One reason is price pressure, which

---

Eccolet

Eccolet began producing shoes in Portugal in the mid-1980s to benefit from the low labour costs there. In 1991, the company started production in Indonesia, where wages were even lower (the cost of labour in Indonesia in 1991 was 10% of that in Portugal, and 2.5% of the Danish level). The use of Indonesia as a production base was made possible by the use of a satellite-based communication system for the transmission of video images and shoe design.

Today, the Eccolet network is based on production of semi-finished goods in Indonesia, final assembly in Portugal, design and quality control in Denmark, supply of raw materials from Eastern Europe, and distribution from the Netherlands.

---

is forcing the value chain from producer to consumer to become more efficient. This forces producers and distributors to a closer co-ordination of their activities in order to cut costs and in some cases this is obtained by producers acquiring distributors. Another reason is that access to the customer may prove to be more valuable than the ability to manufacture the product. In this case producers might see their bargaining position towards distributors to be weakened and thus motivate them to take over distributors.

The pharmaceutical industry in the USA, where producers have taken over distributors, is a good example of how an industry value chain can be changed.

The computer industry also highlights this trend. This industry was once dominated by vertically integrated companies like IBM and DEC, which controlled all value chain elements from R&D to after-sales service. Today, the industry is much more fragmented, with component companies like INTEL, software companies like Microsoft, distribution companies like DELL and hardware companies like IBM and Compaq. While companies in the computer industry are moving away from vertical integration, the reverse is the case in the media business, with the Disney-ABC and Time Warner-Turner mergers. These are simply observations – facts of todays rapidly changing business life.

Competition is now not only between companies but between complete value chains. Some medium-sized companies choose to become members of value chains controlled by big international companies.

There is hidden vertical integration in certain industries. Big retailers like Marks & Spencer in the UK have developed manufacturing expertise so that they can tell their suppliers not only what to do but how to do it in order to maximize earnings. This leaves little doubt as to where the real power lies.

Non-growth/over-capacity

Global manufacturing over-capacity is affecting an increasing number of manufacturing sectors, two examples of which are the chemical and motor industries. One estimate by R. Smith (1994) put the over-capacity in the European motor industry at 30%, and predicts a 10-year period of rationalization. Over-capacity puts pressure on the margins of an industry supply chain, but sometimes with a very uneven distribution. While the overall loss to European car manufacturers in 1993 was GBP 2.6 billion (approximately USD 4,3 billion), the 25 leading component manufacturers made a combined operating profit of GBP 9.4 billion (approximately USD 15,9 billion), according to the economist intelligence unit

The consequences of non-growth and over-capacity are usually unpleasant. Here are four typical scenarios:

1. Some companies try to utilize their capacity by price dumping to increase sales, but causing a price war in the process;
2. Other companies adapt their capacity and cut costs;
3. Sometimes there is official intervention, as has been the case for steel in the EU;
4. The end-result may be an industry shake-out, with some companies going out of business or being taken over by others in an industry restructuring.

Shift in demand patterns

Consumer demand patterns are shifting. One of the reasons is demographic change, with the aging population of the western world. An increasing number of retired people want to live an interesting life, can do so for more years and have the necessary money.

Changing life-styles are also affecting demand. A couple of decades ago, the prospect seemed to be one of less work and more free time for all. The reality is unfortunately very different, with many permanently unemployed and others working longer. We also undertake more do-it-yourself work instead of employing carpenters and electricians.

Consumer expectations are changing too. Several industries have seen a shift in customer requirements from 1) being happy just to be able to get a product to 2) expecting a quality product to 3) expecting a better price-value relationship to 4) expecting tailored products with the price benefit of mass-production. This shift is not a function of market life-cycles. Even in new markets like mobile communication, consumers expect perfect quality.

Market fragmentation, with consumers demanding customized products and services adds to manufacturing complexity. Flexibility in response to changes in customer needs has become important.

Smaller profit windows

In some industries, the profit window, that period in which a company can maintain a unique position and earn better than average profits, is becoming smaller.

One reason for this is the shorter interval between product innovations and, as a consequence, short product life-cycles. In the home-PC market, the interval between new-model introductions has dropped to 6 months. The American company 3M, recognized for its innovation, has a goal where 30% of revenue should come from products less than four years old. In 1994, nearly 7% of 3M revenue came from products launched in that year, according to the Economist (18/11 1995).

Another reason is shorter periods of product exclusivity. In the pharmaceutical industry, a product that comes off patent protection is quickly copied, and sales of the original product decline rapidly. It was reported in the Wall Street Journal (6/12 1995) that Glaxo might lose USD 2 billion of its turnover of approximately USD 14 billion in 1998, because the world's best-selling drug, Zantac, and another drug, Zovirax, were to come off patent in mid-1997.

A third reason is that differentiating advantages are becoming more difficult to sustain. Competitors copy them or develop new advantages. This kind of competition is often seen for instance in consumer electronics.

A further aspect of profit squeeze in some industries is the increase in development and manufacturing costs, which heightens the pressure on revenue generation even further.

Companies facing all these challenges must 1) constantly create products and add-ons, 2) reduce time to market and 3) leverage their products globally to maximize profits within the profit-window.

Technological evolution

Technological evolution is also a force behind change. For example, developments in biotechnology have a major effect on a number of industries, including pharmaceuticals, agriculture, chemicals, environment and food.

Advances in combinatorial chemistry are having a very significant impact on both drug development and product philosophy in the biotechnology industry. It is now possible to identify human genes at far greater speeds than was possible even a few years ago. As a result, new drugs can be tested with computer simulations, and the very emphasis of development is switching from drugs that treat symptoms to drugs that attack the genetic causes of diseases.

IT and biotechnology are both very knowledge-intensive, high-tech industries in which new discoveries fuel discontinuous change. But even in industries where technological innovation is not of such decisive importance, pressure on margins is driving companies to focus on innovation, both in their products and business processes, to create unique advantages. The service industry is a case in point. For instance, the Danish cleaning and maintenance services company ISS, which has world-wide operations, has invested in the development of special cleaning liquids and application techniques to achieve a marketable advantage over its competitors.

2.2 Key strategy focus areas

In this section I shall focus on seven key focus areas for strategic thinking and practice. First, however, a short recapitulation on what strategy should not be.

Back in the 1960s and 1970s, strategy work was seen as a planning exercise, an approach which gave rise to the concept of "strategic planning". Today, most strategy experts do not regard strategy as planning but rather as thinking. In a world in which unexpected change is the rule, you cannot foresee the future in any meaningful way or make plans for the realization of a detailed long term strategy. Nor should strategy formulation/review be merely an annual activity. It should be based upon the unfolding situation and needs of the company.

Equally, strategy formulation should not simply be a senior-management/expert exercise, with conclusions on where the company should be heading communicated top-down to other employees. It should include the collection of bottom-up ideas and perceived opportunities.

And strategy is not only a matter of content, it is just as much an issue of process, including implementation and adjustment.

Last but not least, strategy should not be perceived as simply of long term relevance. Its development should also include short term elements.

Key focus areas for strategy formulation

1. Understanding industry transformation
2. Conceptualizing the core knowledge asset
3. Understanding customer benefits
4. Changing the existing logic
5. Developing an overall direction
6. Developing strategy for both the short and long term
7. Adapting strategy constantly to opportunities and learning

1. Understanding industry transformation

When industries are undergoing transformation, opportunities and the competitive environment also change. To take advantage of new opportunities, a company needs to be prepared, with new products, new knowledge and new skills. But these new resources cannot simply be acquired overnight. It is important to understand the nature of change in a given industry and to exploit this knowledge, identifying areas where resources should be committed. An example might be a distribution company that believed home shopping would become of increasing significance, requiring the company to prepare a solid foundation for entering that retailing sector. This preparatory process may take years, involving experiments with new technology and innovative logistics. It may be that the market will not take off for another five years, but at that stage it would probably be too late. Far-sighted companies will establish in advance the necessary networks and alliances – the competitive infrastructure necessary for success.

2. Conceptualizing the core knowledge asset

As product life-cycles become shorter, it will become important to take a step back and identify a company's real assets. The core asset of any company is the knowledge on which it is built. This is the real root of products, services and revenue. A critical issue for every company is the development of this knowledge and the ability to use it to create business opportunities.

3. Understanding customer benefits

Business opportunities are not only based on knowledge, capabilities and technological miracles. Customers, both existing and potential, play a vital role. They buy a product or service because they want it and believe that the value of the product to them justifies the price. Understanding and assigning an accurate value to the benefits that customers derive from your products is as essential to the process of prioritizing products, service and process innovation as it is to marketing.

4. Changing the existing logic

The ability to see new opportunities requires more than an understanding of industry transformation. It is necessary to be able to think outside a company's normal definition of its business in order to recognize that other opportunities can be *your* opportunities. In other words, challenge established doctrines and think the unthinkable! The most obvious opportunities may not be the most attractive, quite simply because they are obvious to everyone else in the industry as well.

5. Developing an overall direction

The need to be opportunity-driven and flexible does not mean that an overall direction for the company, a mission, is unnecessary. There has to be a clear idea of what the company wants to achieve, and of the basic competencies upon which it must build. There are two reasons for this. First, a shared understanding of an overall direction is necessary to achieve synergy within the company. Second, long term development of capabilities must be based on a perception of what the company should do in the future. The mission should be clear about the ends, but flexible in terms of means.

6. Developing strategies for both the short and long term

When competitive conditions change fundamentally and rapidly, even within the space of a couple of years, strategy becomes important in the short term as well. The goal in the short term is to constantly improve the company's position, for example through special promotions and by targeting special customer groups. In the longer term, on the other hand, the goal is to change the rules of the game, foresee how these will change and to see completely new games (new products, new markets, new industries).

7. Constantly adapting strategies to opportunities and learning

In a changing world, formulating a successful strategy depends to a significant degree on learning by experimenting with new directions, and on recognizing opportunities that suddenly crystallize during that process.

2.3 The new wave of strategy thinking

The authors of strategy books now being published frequently mention the shortcomings of other experts. There is no longer any clear leader in business strategy theory, as had been the case with Michael Porter in the 1980s. Proponents of strategy are taking a long hard look at the field. A revolution is brewing.

I shall now present ideas and concepts that address the issues raised earlier in this chapter. These concepts and ideas are primarily based upon the work of strategy thinkers published within the last five years. First, however, I will look briefly at some of the main schools of thought within business strategy.

The schools of thought within business strategy

Leading thinkers in business strategy have traditionally been divided into two groups, according to whether they adopted a positioning approach or a resource-based approach.

The positioning approach is represented, among others, by Michael Porter, and his thoughts on a company's need to adapt as effectively as possible to the environment, industry and market. This line of thinking focuses on understanding a company's industry and the drivers of profitability in it. Strategy development focuses mostly on the "outside-in". The approach is adaptive in nature.

The resource-based approach is a later wave of thought represented by, for instance, Prahalad and Hamel. It focuses on a company's own competencies and capabilities as the starting point for strategy development. This "inside-out" approach is rooted in the belief that a company needs to change the rules of the competitive game within its industry, and can do so if it develops unique capabilities and competencies.

There is in fact also a third line of thought that differs from both the above schools, because it focuses less on the origins of strategy content and more on the process of strategy development. This third approach could be called the *learning-based approach,* advocated by Henry Mintzberg. Its supporters argue that strategy should not be taught (by academia, consultants and others) in a prescriptive manner but is, and should be, formed gradually through learning.

Companies, they say, very seldom achieve their intended strategies. This is good because it indicates that strategy is adapted to take into account opportunities that arise and other events that occur in the market. This school of thought focuses more on the organizational issues of strategy than on content.

The argument is that there are a lot of opportunities in the market and many good strategies are available to exploit them. The problem is to turn these opportunities into business success. It is rather like having a PC and a broad range of software. The potential to exploit the PC's power is enormous, but few people have the ability to utilize such potential fully. Indeed, many only use the PC as an advanced typewriter.

The concepts and thoughts selected for consideration in this chapter build on all three lines of thought, and are primarily intended to stimulate strategic thinking, the activity that takes place before major decisions are made.

I do not believe in generally applicable recipes for success in business. Nothing can be a substitute for the ability of a company's employees to generate business ideas based upon what is going on in the market, among innovative companies and in the world of technology.

I do, however, believe that effective strategic thinking can be stimulated by developing a framework for the process, adapted to the specific situation of a given company.

Such a framework could, for example, be based on the "building blocks" listed in the chart (see page 34), which are considered in more detail below.

Obtaining market insight and foresight

A company's decisions regarding products and markets rests to some degree on insight, and partly on foresight. "Insight" I define as an understanding of the present situation and how it has evolved, while "foresight" is a perception of the future. Both are important in strategy work, but the latter has, in our experience, been neglected in strategy practice in recent years.

Building blocks of dynamic strategy

- Obtaining market insight and foresight
- Utilizing a company's competencies
- Determining the value a company wants to provide
- Reinventing the business and the competitive rules
- Developing a guiding strategic intent
- Developing strategy as a dynamic game
- Capitalizing on opportunities and learning

Foresight is important because it involves understanding future development, though not only in the form of incremental change, such as the increase in electronic-chip capacity, which is an often-used example.

Foresight can also be used to predict discontinuous change in competitive conditions. Points at which the fundamental rules of the competitive game in an industry change are called *breakpoints*. Paul Strebel (1992) described in an interesting way how the computer industry has been characterized by such breakpoints. The chart below shows these shifts in a simplified form.

Competitive shifts within the personal computer industry

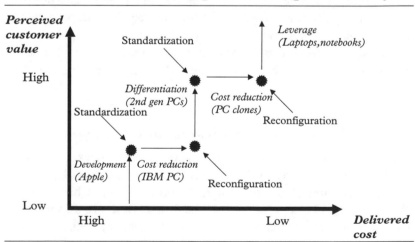

Source: P. Strebel, "breakpoints", 1992

The chart suggests that during the evolution of the personal computer industry there has been a shift in emphasis away from delivered cost towards perceived product value, though both have been in constant focus and have improved simultaneously.

A breakpoint occurs when there is a shift in competitive practice, e.g. a) from competition over costs to competition based on quality/value, b) from competition on products to competition on service, or c) from competition in manufacturing to competition in distribution. Unfortunately, many companies don't have the ability to create breakpoints. Even worse, many fail to exploit breakpoints when they do occur. The consequences for companies that do not see these breakpoints, or see them too late, can be catastrophic.

Establishing foresight must include not only the discussion of shifts, like the ones described above, but also the development of an understanding of what drives these shifts. The reason for a competitive shift may be diminishing returns from trying to reduce costs or increase value, or it could be an external factor, such as a trend in the economic cycle. The trick is to foresee when the market is ready for a breakpoint, and then to create it. However, it is worth noting that, if you have a niche, you may be able to protect yourself from such competitive shifts, at least to some degree.

The concept underlying the above chart can be used to plot the moves (and thus the logic) of individual competitors. Competitor analysis is all too often an exercise in which a competitor's current strengths and weaknesses are measured. This only provides a static picture. Prahalad and Hamel (1994) compared this to a snapshot of a moving car. The photograph offers little information about the car's direction, and nothing about the mentality of the driver.

Industry foresight is a more qualitative exercise during which a picture of the future is formed. It should be built upon a deep understanding of the trends or forces that are affecting the industry concerned. These forces may relate to changes in technology, sociology, politics or demography. A good question to address is which trends could most radically influence a given company's business, in terms of both opportunities and threats.

Prahalad and Hamel (1994) p. 81-105, suggest the following principles be applied in order to discover and develop foresight:

- Don't extrapolate the industry of today, especially using the boundaries of the existing industry as limitations. Rather, base your

views of the future on the value you provide and the core
strengths on which you base your business.
* Be curious about what new technologies can do for your industry.
* Be open to predictions – even made by people you normally don't
  listen to.
* Be patient. Foresight doesn't materialize on a given day. It will
  develop over time.
* Look for analogies among developments in other industries.

Utilizing a company's competencies

Competitive advantage is not derived from physical assets like products or plants. These can be copied or outperformed. It comes from
skills, experience, know-how or market intelligence which is difficult
to copy.

A company's ability to develop, produce and sell products or services essentially rests on the skills, technology and knowledge of how
to do things. Core competence is a collection of elements in these
categories that are critical to a company's competitive success. In
other words, not all competencies are core. According to Prahalad
and Hamel (1994), core competencies:

1. deliver a disproportionate contribution to customer benefit (or
   value);
2. differentiate the company from its competitors;
3. can be extended to other product applications.

Below is an example of how a core competence fits into the general picture for a particular company, Federal Express:

Package-tracking at Federal Express is a good example of how a
particular core competence fits into the general picture. This particular competence is essential to delivering the fundamental value to
the customer, which is on-time delivery. Package-tracking competence is not unique to Federal Express, but is mastered there.

Core competencies are not the same as competitive advantages or
critical success factors. For instance, a patent can be a source of
competitive advantage, but is not in itself a core competence. A
company's core competencies can be compared to the roots of a
tree. They are the fundamental elements that a business relies on.
They are the source of the company's key products.

Core competencies, capabilities and skills

Example: Federal Express	
Value provided:	On-time delivery
	↓
Capability:	Logistics management
	↓
Core competency:	Package tracking
	↓
Skills:	Linear programming
	↓
Supporting technologies:	Bar-coding, wireless communication

The following two lessons for strategy development embody the concept of core competencies:

A. The concept implies a way of looking at business expansion by viewing core competencies as a source of new products. This is eminently practiced by Japanese companies like Honda and Sony. They seem to have a very broad product scope, but the products are closely tied together because they rely on the same core competencies. Naturally, this element of "diversification" involves risks. For example, in the case of Honda, cars are quite different from motorcycles in terms of consumer demands.

B. The core competencies concept could suggest that all competencies that are not core should be outsourced. Performing functions not critical to the company or in which it does not achieve a world-class standard makes it vulnerable, because a competitor could exploit this weak spot. This philosophy has been followed by many companies, leading to a wave of outsourcing and the formation of networked companies in industries like textiles, shoes and computers.

There are various ways in which competencies can be developed or acquired on favorable terms. Alliances with other companies or universities possessing skills or knowledge in the required area are one effective solution.

This emphasis on competencies – essentially knowledge – as a core asset makes it necessary for companies to think about how to

---

Virtual integration – Celltech

Outsourcing, or virtual integration, is a very strong force in the bio-tech industry. Bio-tech companies partner with academia for discovery, and with pharmaceutical companies for marketing, distribution and sales.

The UK bio-tech company Celltech has entered into a series of deals with major pharmaceutical companies. One of these deals is with the US pharmaceutical company Merck. The two partners have signed an agreement relating to a particular asthma treatment. Celltech will receive payments from Merck relating to its progress in developing the treatment through the clinical phases. Merck has the marketing rights to any end-products and Celltech will receive a royalty.

---

develop, maintain, protect and value them. The first step, however, is to discover these competencies. This is not easy, because we tend to focus more on visible strengths, such as physical assets, financial assets and individuals. Identifying invisible assets demands an ability to understand the inner workings of a company and its business.

An excellent example of the value of competencies was provided by the US company Netscape (which produces a highly successful Internet browser) in the early stages of the Internet "explosion". In December 1995, this company was traded on the NASDAQ exchange at 48 times its forecast 1996 sales and 538 times its forecast 1996 earnings. At around the same time, Microsoft, the world's biggest software company, was being traded at 35 times realized 1995 earnings.

There are many companies that are not fully capitalizing on their core competencies because they are not effective in applying them to new products, or if they do, they may not be effective in their marketing of the new product. A new business idea has to go through many phases: idea ⇒ product concept ⇒ production ⇒ marketing/sales ⇒ customer. Each step represents a hurdle at which the idea may fall by the wayside.

Determining the value a company wants to provide

It has been an accepted philosophy for many years that companies should be customer-driven, not product-driven. They should produce what customers want rather than simply offering customers what they happen to produce. The logic behind this is clear: If you want to make customers happy, give them what they want or what they can benefit from, so that they obtain maximum satisfaction from your products. But for many companies this is easier said than done, because:

1. It can be difficult to discover what customers really want;
2. You cannot be all things to all customers, so you have to choose customer segments and the benefits you want to provide;
3. Changes in products and services may be needed;
4. Changing your delivery system may also be required.

It also needs to be pointed out at this juncture that any change in strategy must be clearly communicated to customers, with an emphasis on benefits rather than product features. Business thinkers like Treacy & Wiersma (1995) place special emphasis on the value a customer receives and the manner in which it is provided. Companies need to develop and communicate clear *value propositions* that specify which customers they want to serve, the benefits they provide and at what price. Toys R Us, for example, offers customers in urban areas lowest prices and hassle-free service, based on a broad selection.

Customers pick the supplier with the most attractive benefit/cost combination. The benefit comes from elements like product performance and durability, purchase convenience and product range. The cost is related to acquiring the product (price, financing) and using the product. The customer subjectively weighs these elements against each other before making the buy/re-buy decision.

Treacy & Wiersma suggest that companies should pick one of three generic value propositions (value disciplines):

1. The best total cost (best price, hassle-free service), like McDonald's;
2. The best product (best performance), like NIKE;
3. The best solution (tailored, individual service), like Harrods.

The trick is to excel in one area while maintaining acceptable levels in the others.

To develop a value proposition you need to choose the customers you want to serve and the value you want to supply them with. This demands clever market segmentation. Segmenting a market according to geographical, demographic or economic variables is not that difficult, because it can often be supported by specific statistical data. Segmentation of a market according to customer needs or benefits is much more difficult, because the data is seldom available. One approach is to use the bottom-up method, examining a typical customer, identifying the value s/he wants, and then looking for others like him/her.

To determine the benefits you want to provide, you also need to put yourself into your customers' shoes. You need to understand the kind of benefits that could make their lives easier and/or better. SmithKline Beecham has, according to the Danish newspaper Børsen (15/9 1995), changed its value proposition on the basis of an understanding of their direct customers:

Focusing on value – SmithKline Beecham

The pharmaceutical industry all over the world has been under pressure in recent years because governments want to cut health-care costs. This has led pharmaceutical companies to try to change from being providers of drugs to providers of effective disease treatments, with a focus on the costs and benefits of disease treatment.

The UK pharmaceutical company SmithKline Beecham has offered the Danish Government an opportunity to share its experience with managed health care. A US managed-care company owned by SmithKline Beecham has collected data on disease management from 20 million customers, which has provided a unique insight into the effectiveness of various medicines and treatments.

In a business-to-business environment, to understand your direct customers' situation, you also need to understand what drives their customers. In fact, the key is to understand what determines *end-user satisfaction*. In this way you see yourself as part of a value chain competing with other value chains. Some companies segment both their immediate customers and customers further down the value chain, such as the distribution system used to reach the end-user, and obtain interesting new business-development perspectives as a result.

Just as important as developing the value proposition is designing an operating model (including core processes, structure and skills) that makes it possible for a company to deliver value profitably. This could be called the "profit engine" of a company, a topic to which I shall revert later.

Re-inventing the business, and competitive rules

Those who have worked in sales know that selling is a lot easier if your product or service is a little bit different from your competitors'. Creating small advantages is essential for every company. On a larger scale, developments in such areas as information technology provide opportunities to create new advantages, or even to re-invent an industry. "Re-invention" involves changing an industry's competitive rules, developing completely new products, or changing the fundamental financial relationships between companies in a value chain. Prahalad & Hamel (1989) provided recommendations on competitive innovation and D'Aveni (1994) has offered recommendations on how to create competitive disruption.

The principles of *competitive innovation* listed above are based on the strategies used by Japanese companies for global expansion, often rivaling against much bigger competitors. The principles are

Searching for creative strategies

Competitive innovation	Competitive disruption
• Build layers of advantages (change competitive arena) • Search for loose bricks (attack undefended segments) • Change business concept (do not accept the leader's definition of how business is done) • Make alliances to overcome disadvantages	• Find new ways to improve customer satisfaction • Find opportunities through understanding trends of change • Ability to move quickly • Ability to surprise • Shift the rules of the game • Strategic market communication • Attack with several competitive weapons simultaneously

Source : Prahalad & Hamel (1989). D'Aveni (1994) p. 243-249

based upon the sound logic that, if you are a small challenger, do not try to play by the rules of larger competitors. To gain market share you must find the weak spots of competitors and build on your own strengths and advantages. Canon successfully expanded its photocopier business in the USA by using competitive innovation, as reported by Prahalad and Hamel (1989) and Ghoshal (1992).

Changing a business logic – the case of Canon

When Canon entered the copier business in the 1970s, it changed the logic of how to run a copier business.

The dominant player, with a 93% market share in 1970, was Xerox, which offered a very broad range of copiers, with frequent introductions of new models. These machines were costly, so Xerox began leasing machines, which included service agreements and paper supplies. Sales were conducted through an extensive direct-sales organization which typically targeted central staff functions, because the Xerox concept was based upon centralizing copying with its big machines.

Canon entered the market with smaller, cheaper machines for decentralized copy locations. These products were distributed through office-product dealers, who were also made responsible for service. Canon thus avoided the cost of establishing a large sales and service network. Copy machines were simply sold, not leased, so Canon also avoided the cost of leasing.

Canon later became leader of the small offices market that had been ignored by Xerox, by aggressive sales to this segment with a new line of products called personal copiers. Xerox had difficulties in responding because its business set-up (cost-structure) was designed for a specific type of business and could not easily be changed.

The principles of *competitive disruption* in the above chart illustrate how temporary advantage can be created by combining a vision for disruption with the capabilities necessary for disruption, and by obtaining advantage through tactics. A vision for disruption might be based on identifying ways in which customer satisfaction can be improved, and by understanding the opportunities available through changes in technology and lifestyle. The two fundamental capabilities necessary to create disruption are speed and surprise. Finally, competitive disruption should be delivered by constantly changing the rules of the game, using market communication to attract customers or confuse competitors, as well as attacking with several weapons simultaneously, e.g. launching a new, improved product at a lower price.

To create competitive innovation or disruption it is necessary to *"learn to forget"*, i.e. to ignore the past. Many managers build their managerial practice on what they have learned personally and from successful companies in the same industry. But building on your own experience and the experiences of others puts a box around you. When new opportunities occur or an industry is changing, past experience can become a limiting element, making it difficult to see the innovative actions that could be possible. This is why it is important to have employees with different backgrounds and experience. The sometimes limited usefulness of past experience also suggests that a company's intellectual capital has to be written off rather quickly, and that it is essential to invest in the creation of new intellectual capital.

Developing a guiding strategic intent

One of the central philosophies of strategic planning was to create consistency between a company's goals and its means. This logic may have produced consistent plans, but it also resulted in inflexibility. A new view is emerging, illustrated in the chart page 44. It is based upon the ideas of the various strategy experts mentioned in this report.

The main principle of the strategy pyramid was to make a company's mission and vision operational by gradually detailing ends and means. According to this principle, the company vision should be a broad description of how the company should look in the future, while the action plans should be a much more detailed description and specification of what the company should do in the short term. But phrases like "company mission" (Why do we exist?) and "company vision" (What should we look like in 10 years?) have become somewhat problematic. They have been misused and associated with popular phrases that nobody believed in. Visions were seldom realized and diverted attention away from real day-to-day problems. This difficulty can often be traced back to the vision of the future

The strategy logic

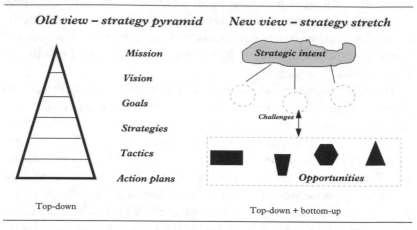

Old view – strategy pyramid	New view – strategy stretch
Mission	Strategic intent
Vision	
Goals	
Strategies	Challenges
Tactics	Opportunities
Action plans	
Top-down	Top-down + bottom-up

being too vague, and to an inability to define and implement the desired change that could have linked the future with the present.

What is a strategic intent?

In a changing world, there is nevertheless good reason for companies to have a vision of what they should look like in the future. A *strategic intent* is a company's vision of what it wants to achieve in the long term. It encompasses the "intellectual" idea (represented in the above chart by a free-form shape) of a company's ultimate purpose and envisions a desired leadership position. The strategic intent must convey a significant "stretch" for the company, a sense of direction, discovery and opportunity that can be conveyed as worthwhile to all employees. Examples of expressions of strategic intent would be Coca Cola's dream of putting a Coke within arm's reach of every consumer in the world, and President Kennedy's dream of putting a man on the moon before the Soviet Union.

Strategic intent should specify those factors critical to success in the future, in other words, the key competitive factors. It must be also be accompanied by intermediate goals against which company achievements can be measured. It should also develop and mature with time. It cannot be developed in a one-day strategy session. Strategic intent is different from traditional missions, visions and goals. In our experience, the allocation of time between long term and short term issues in strategy work is very much proportional to their share of the strategy pyramid, since action plans are allotted a considerable amount of time, while vision and mission are given less. This is probably one of the reasons why company visions often lack discovery, opportunity and purpose, the critical elements of strategic intent.

Strategic intent must be based on a vision of how the future will look in 10-15 years. Aspects include future demand, customers, products and competitor supply systems etc. It is especially important to create a picture of the future customer daily life, his/her needs and the success factors required for meeting these needs. Any view of the future must include *discovery* and *detection of opportunity*. These serve as platforms for developing strategic intent. Forecasts and predictions must be blended with imagination that is detached from today's world. It is particularly important to describe discontinuities, any anticipated fundamental changes from the world of today.

A powerful way to explain your view of the future and your intent within that future is the video medium. It is much easier to discuss and create understanding of the future if you make it visual, rather than just using words. The US company Apple produced a video in which it showed the home of the future, with an intelligent Apple "servant" managing various functions. Apple's vision is built on a perception of trends in lifestyles and technology.

As stressed earlier, the logic, uniqueness and discovery that make intent come to life for employees are vitally important. They have to understand, believe and live according to the strategic intent. The Body Shop is based on a logic that cosmetics can be pure and natural, and do not need to be packaged and marketed in a fancy way. The Danish company ISS is built on a logic that it is a building-maintenance company, not a cleaning company.

One of the points that various strategy experts make is that strategic intent should not focus so much on today's problems, which are normally dealt with by company missions and visions, but rather on *tomorrow's opportunities*. Basically, strategy should be a *stretch exercise,* not a fit exercise, so that the end-result is not possible today and lies beyond the present planning period. To achieve great things, you need ambitious visions. And it does not matter that the road to that vision cannot be laid out in detail. It is the direction that counts.

Reaching for the intent – challenges and opportunities

Prahalad and Hamel compare the realization of strategic intent to a marathon run in 400-meter stages. Ignore what the terrain looks like 30 kilometers on, just concentrate on the next 400 meters and, when you have conquered that terrain, concentrate on the next 400 meters. You cannot lay out a detailed plan for the realization of intent. There are too many elements of uncertainty and the future keeps changing! Strategic intent should convey a sense of direction that can be used to identify major tasks.

A limited number of *challenges* should be defined each year, necessary steps towards realizing a given strategic intent. Though a company may have a vision of the path to the future, the challenges on the road and the road's direction may well change along the way. The challenges met by the Japanese company Komatsu evolved over a 20-year period, from protecting its home-market by reducing costs and building exports to creating new products and markets. Challenges should be specific, such as reducing time to market to 6 months, so that it is easy to monitor whether targets are achieved. Challenges also need to be split into a number of different projects.

The last element in the new strategy model is *opportunities* that arise or crystallize on a continuous basis. Every company meets new opportunities (and threats) daily. An employee discovers an opportunity to sell a current product in a new market segment, for example, or a competitor suddenly goes up for sale. Such opportunities do not wait for the next strategy meeting. Opportunities may shape new challenges and influence strategic intent. They may also be defined as short term projects intended to improve the performance of the present business set-up.

Developing strategy as a dynamic game

In a world of constant change, competitive advantage does not last and becomes increasingly difficult to sustain. Many companies have devoted themselves to following a low-cost, differentiation or focus strategy, as suggested by Porter. The chart in the section on market insight, showing competitive developments in the personal computer industry, provides a clear indication of the danger inherent in blindly focusing on just one of these strategies.

In broader terms, research by Richard D'Aveni shows that companies must strive to continuously create new advantages. Competition often evolves as shown in this chart.

How competitive battles evolve in a market

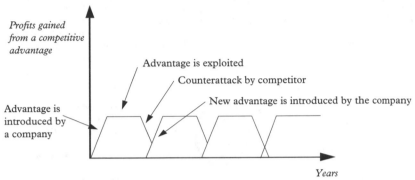

Source : R. D'Aveni (1994) p. 12

The US company American Airlines developed a competitive edge by creating a series of new advantages between 1981 and 1992:

Advantage 1 Launch of frequent flyer program
Advantage 2 Extend frequent flyer program to include car rental mileage and hotel
Advantage 3 Frequent flyer miles to be used in various shops etc.
Advantage 4 New fare structure

Each advantage has its own life-cycle, with a length that depends on how difficult it is to copy.

The purpose of strategy is to destroy the status quo, not to optimize a company's situation within it. This even applies to the market leader, because no advantage lasts. Strategy is dynamic and relative, in the sense that you are only a low-cost producer as long as there is somebody else who is producing at higher costs.

All strategic moves within an industry will be followed by reaction, which is why companies must project their competitors' reactions when discussing alternative strategy options. The keys to the competitive game are flexibility, adaptability and an ability to re-invent both the competitive rules and the game itself. Strategy consists of both a short term and a long term game, as illustrated in the chart page 48.

The strategy game in a market

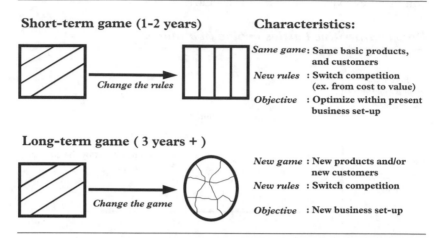

Short-term game (1-2 years)

Change the rules

Long-term game (3 years +)

Change the game

Characteristics:

Same game: Same basic products, and customers

New rules : Switch competition (ex. from cost to value)

Objective : Optimize within present business set-up

New game : New products and/or new customers

New rules : Switch competition

Objective : New business set-up

In its most simple form, the *short term game* consists of simply doing better, such as constantly improving prices or quality and capitalizing on opportunities. In the short term, companies even try to change the rules of the game by switching from price competition to product innovation competition. Competition on price (cost) and quality (innovation) are two variations on the competitive theme. Today these themes are sophisticated. Price competition also becomes competition for resources, and competition based on innovation also becomes competing for speed, e.g. being first in the market.

The short term game can involve developing a short term plan with a series of competitive moves to increase short term market share, as illustrated by the example below, Churchill (1995).

Another goal of the short term game is, or should be, to optimize the use of a company's current profit-engine or business set-up. A profit-engine includes a company's business definition (segments, products, customer benefits, industry role), delivery system (processes, organization, culture), source of profits and key success factors. Profit-engines have a life-cycle, just like a product, and should be changed before they lose steam, or when a new engine can produce even better results.

The purpose of the *long term game* is to build a company according to its strategic intent. This may involve the creation of complete-

---

Short term plan for competitive disruption
– America On-line

America On-Line is the leading US on-line services company, with already more than 1.5 million subscribers, and growing very fast in terms of both subscribers and content. America On-Line has various information channels, entertainment, e-mail services and Internet access.

By the end of 1994, America On-Line had overtaken Prodigy and CompuServe, but was facing a threat from Microsoft's new MSN network. The new president of America On-Line services, Ted Leonsis, developed an umbrella strategy, including offensive moves in several areas, to position America On-Line as the only consumer alternative to Microsoft.

The umbrella strategy included agreements with marketing partners and content providers, branding of the individual information channels, acquisition of an Internet company, launch of an Internet shopping network, and a series of tactical announcements aimed at portraying Microsoft as the "big bad wolf" and America On-Line as the fast-growing, consumer-friendly service provider. The strategy was to be carried out over a six-month period, with the specific purpose of obtaining 5 million subscribers ahead of Microsoft – a fight for vast future revenue opportunities.

---

ly new services and the attraction of new types of customers. A completely new business set-up may be needed.

The difficulty is that companies have to manage both the short term and long term games at the same time. It is like badminton. The short term game, winning the point, constantly puts you into new situations and you have to vary your game to surprise your opponent. You must also have a long term strategy for winning the match, which is developed during the match. This strategy could be to move the game all over the court, because you believe your condition is better than your opponent's and s/he will tire more quickly. Sun Tzu, a military strategist who lived about 3,000 years ago, put it this way: All men can see the tactics whereby I conquer, but what none can see is the strategy out of which great victory is evolved.

Capitalizing on opportunities and learning

Management is different from leadership, just as strategy creation is different from planning. According to Kotter (1990), management is making sure that targets are met through action plans, resource allocation, follow-up procedures and systems. Leadership is about creating change, setting a new direction and institutionalizing opportunity-driven mechanisms. Both management and leadership are necessary.

Short term plans without direction are as bad as long term visions without short term action plans and budgets. But a detailed five-year business plan mixing the two often results in inflexibility, or at least waste of paper, because such plans can be difficult to maintain and may not be appropriate at any given time.

The CEO is guardian of the strategic intent, coach, and facilitator of the organizational environment that makes it possible for employees to perform optimally. Peter Senge compares a company to a ship. In his view, the CEO's most important role is not that of captain or navigator, but of ship designer. The ship designer, he says, is the most influential. The captain can only operate within the limits and potential the designer has provided.

Top management devises, communicates and motivates a company's strategic intent, basing this on input from various people inside and outside the company. As discussed earlier, strategic intent should take the form of a number of corporate challenges, specified as short term projects and opportunities. Such opportunities could naturally evolve into "big business", but direction does not emerge solely from opportunities that employees chase or create.

Strategic intent cannot be planned all in advance. It must evolve on the basis of experience during its implementation. Separating strategy creation from strategy implementation by using corporate planners or consultants for the former activity is thus a hindrance to the evolution of a successful strategy. Linking creation and implementation supports the overall process, and thus a strategy emerges and evolves. This view is further supported by the need for strategy to change constantly in order to contend with external turbulence.

Experimenting with new strategies is important. In today's fast-changing world, a company does not simply undertake a five-year product-development project and then test the finished product at the end of the process. Rapid prototyping is now used for both products and business concepts. Constant testing, adaptation and building on what is found to be successful with customers is the way ahead, especially when a company is trying to re-invent the value provided, or the way it is produced and delivered.

Creating opportunities by experimenting – Arovit Petfood

Arovit Petfood is a rapidly growing, profitable, medium-sized Danish company with a turnover of just below USD 100 million.

Arovit's traditional business was the production of foodstuffs used by fur farms. A crisis in the fur industry led to a search for alternative products and markets in which the company's product and processing know-how could be used. Arovit chose to move into pet food, one of the few growth markets in daily consumer goods.

After some years in the pet food business, Arovit faced increasingly tough competition from international brand giants like Master Foods and Nestlé. Private-label marketing was a growing trend at the time, so Arovit explored opportunities in selling private-label pet food to European supermarket chains. By working closely together with supermarket chains like Marks & Spencer, and being flexible in relation to its customers' demands, Arovit has succeeded in quadrupling revenues since the late-1980s.

Mintzberg says that corporate planners should not be involved in strategy formation, but should simply provide support, analyzing issues and trends, and evaluating consequences. They should focus attention on current issues, rather than attempt to direct a future course. At 3M, those implementing strategy are also strategy creators, because employees are allowed to chase business opportunities they find.

The best strategies are often fueled by learning about customers. Ideas for new strategies can pop up as the result of a particular customer experience. Such potential opportunities cannot be programmed into the agenda for an annual strategy session.

Opportunities can, however, be detected or created before they emerge, by asking very simple questions, e.g.:

What are the trends that will change our industry?
What are our customers dissatisfied with?
What will the daily life of our customers look like in 10 years?

Working with the trends that drive changes in an industry must not only rely upon scenarios, forecasts and statements by experts. A company's own concept of what the future will hold is also vital input, not least because it is the only unique element in the equation. It is also important to note that it is necessary to think about products that could be valuable to customers, not just those products and services they ask for. Customers do not necessarily know what is technologically possible, and must therefore be given guidance.

In general, creativity and the detection of new opportunities can often be stimulated by being curious or asking impossible questions. Nicholas Hayek, the creator of Swatch, asked the impossible question, "Why cannot an attractive low-cost, high quality watch be designed and made in Switzerland?" This question was considered impossible because of high production costs in Switzerland, and domination of the low-cost end of the market by Japanese companies. What happened thereafter is a well-known success story.

2.4 Strategy and common business sense

Too often, strategy is linked to sophisticated intellectual processes run by big planning staffs with MBAs. But it does not need to be this way. In fact, some of the elements in such processes may well help to dampen essential aspects of strategic thinking. You can be an excellent strategist without knowing the word "strategy", just as you can be an excellent business manager without graduating from a business school.

Good strategists may have certain personality traits in common, like curiosity, creativity, intuition and drive. But there are also some very basic principles linked to strategic thinking, action and learning, and the interaction between these, that can improve the success of strategic decisions. These principles could be termed "common business sense".

In concluding this section of the book, I offer the following "common business sense" principles as ways of improving the success of strategic decisions.

The essential elements of strategy

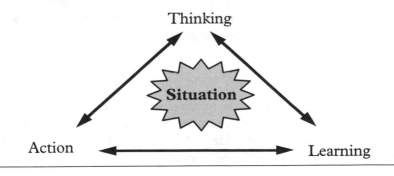

Strategic thinking

1. Look behind the symptoms

You know when you are ill because you experience various symptoms. You also know that the treatment of symptoms does not cure illness. Treating symptoms and going after superficial opportunities are common in the business world. Good strategic thinking, on the other hand, involves attacking the causes of problems and understanding the drivers of new opportunities. To do this, one needs to ask questions that will reveal possible causes, their interaction and effect, and then analyze the answers. This basic process is often neglected, perhaps because of the pressure to find quick solutions.

2. Combine intuition and data

Making decisions purely on the basis of intuition can be dangerous, just as decisions based purely upon analysis can result in no new ideas. But carrying out the two processes separately and then combining them can result in strategies that are both realistic and creative.

3. Recognize the value of synergy

Some good strategists we have met possess an ability to see business opportunities as combinations of elements from a number of areas. For example, they might link customer needs, technology, product, positioning and pricing to create a new business idea. Often we can only see clearly in certain areas. This potential deficiency can be eliminated by creating a platform for synergy, by putting people with different backgrounds together in group sessions.

4. Live the life of the customer

Many great business successes have resulted from someone having a good understanding of the customer's needs and desires. Customers can act as catalysts of new ideas, for instance by being invited to group sessions. Successful strategies are seldom created in an ivory tower.

5. Balance the short and long term

Strategy is not only about visions of the future. Nor is it only about increasing profits next year. It is both. Long term projects intended to build up the business over the next five years are just as necessary as activities to create next year's advantage.

Strategic action

6. Make a choice

Choosing a new strategy and deciding to implement it can be very difficult, because it almost always includes consequences that someone does not like. Disagreement usually starts in the top-management group. The result may be no decision or a bad compromise. This can be dangerous if a company is faced with a radically changing situation and needs to take immediate action.

7. Take risks

New strategies often involve taking risks, particularly if you are moving into new territory. But increasing revenue, market share or profit usually involves a degree of risk.

8. Sell the new strategy

Any new strategy is worth nothing if management does not have the ability to sell it to the company's close stakeholders, which are employees, customers and bankers. This selling process can be difficult if the new strategy is a major shift in direction for the company. There are bound to be skeptics.

An obvious persuasion technique is to create a sense of crisis, to assert that change is essential for the company to survive and prosper. A less effective solution, given that skeptics usually base their doubts on an innate conservatism, is to make the goal to be achieved by change look more attractive than the present situation.

9. Calculate the reactions

When launched, a new strategy will provoke reactions, both internally and from competitors. These reactions may kill the strategy if you have not already thought through a way to cope with them.

10. Get the timing right

Timing is everything. A good strategy launched at the wrong time may fail. An organization may not be ready or the market may not be ready. Good timing is usually based on a combination of intuition and industry foresight.

11. Acquire the appropriate resources

The cost of implementing a new strategy is often larger than expected. If you have limited resources, you must ensure that you do not choose a strategy that will stretch your resources to the limit over a given period.

Strategic learning

12. Undertake strategic control

Controlling a strategy is necessary, so that it can be modified and the chances of success increased. Strategic control should be based not only on numbers but also on initial reactions and comments from customers and employees.

13. Experiment

Implementing a new strategy on a small scale, such as by introducing a new service to a limited customer group, can provide very useful information. Experimenting reduces risk, especially if the company is trying to re-invent the way things are done in an industry.

14. Constantly refine the strategy

In an ever-changing world, a strategy should constantly be modified and changed to keep up with new opportunities and new threats. This is why some companies have moved away from big annual strategy sessions to more creative meetings, perhaps quarterly or whenever the need is felt.

15. Learn from mistakes

When implementing a new strategy, not everything works. The entire strategy may even be a fiasco. It is necessary to recognize failure. The longer you try to cover up failure, the more damage it can do. The problem is to know when something is a real mistake. Many successes have been born out of projects where all except a few had lost faith. As long as there is drive and progress (not necessarily measured in financial terms) there may be good reason for continuing along a certain course. Mistakes can provide valuable insights, if accurately analyzed, such as into customer mentality.

Part Tree

Case stories

- *Dandy (Denmark)*

- *Politiken (Denmark)*

- *Infogrames (France)*

- *Dru (Holland)*

- *Jansen Group (Holland)*

3.1 Dandy[1]
Acting big in new markets

Introduction

This case study recounts how the chewing-gum manufacturer Dandy, after the fall of the Iron Curtain, changed its strategic focus away from the very competitive West European market to developing new opportunities in Eastern Europe. It did so by ignoring one of the traditional rules: "Don't market a product before it is available to customers." In the process, Dandy almost doubled turnover from DKK 731 million (approximately USD 130 million) in 1992 to DKK 1.411 billion (approximately USD 255 million) in 1995, and more than trebled profits from DKK 31 million (approximately USD 5 million) in 1992 to DKK 134 million (approximately USD 22 million) in 1995.

Lars Funder, CEO for Dandy, offered the following perspective on Dandy's success: "The future belongs to small, flexible and focused companies that can react quickly when opportunities arise and which can adapt business philosophy, products and delivery systems to the particular situation. A necessary condition, though, is that the organization is tuned for top performance. This was exactly Dandy's situation in 1992."

Company history/profile

Dandy was founded in 1915 as a confectionery business. Production of chewing-gum began in 1927. The company operated solely in the domestic market until shortly after 1945, when it had to export to be able to import raw materials. The post-war American cultural influence fueled an average annual growth of 20% until the late 1970s. Dandy's main brand, Stimorol®, was introduced in 1956, and Dandy acquired the dental chewing-gum company Fertin in 1978.

---

1. Casework completed in 1996

During the 1980s, having built up excess production capacity, Dandy signed an agreement with Kraft Jacobs Suchard to produce Hollywood chewing-gum. In the early 1990s, Dandy's marketing strategy shifted fundamentally towards a centralized focus on building Stimorol. This shift was one of the foundation stones for the growth of business in Eastern Europe, with a remarkable effect on the company's key figures.

DANDY – key figures

	1986	1987	1988	1989	1990	1991	1992	1993	1994	1995
Turnover	428	489	488	576	629	696	731	813	1230	1411
Pretax profit	11	-2	56	52	48	18	31	54	101	134
Equity	78	78	137	174	210	222	226	256	328	400

Source : Dandy   *All figures in DKK millions*

Just over 50% of Dandy sales are currently linked to Stimorol, about 30% to the dental chewing-gums Dirol® and V6®, and 20% to own-label sales. Production is mainly in Denmark, but a new factory in Russia is planned and there are small joint-ventures in Zimbabwe and Botswana.

Production, product development, quality control, human resources, financial accounting and control are centralized. Four profit-center business units are primarily concerned with sales and marketing:

Stimorol Chewing Gum A/S (Western Europe, the Stimorol brand);
Dandy Chewing Gum A/S (other markets except Russia, the Dirol brand);
Fertin A/S (dental chewing-gum, with distribution through pharmacies, the V6 brand);
Russian brands division (the Russian market).

Dandy is still a family-owned company, although the family has not been involved in day-to-day operations since 1991.

The chewing-gum market

Although classed as a confectionery product, chewing-gum is not in competition with other forms of confectionery. This market can be divided into four generic segments:

Chewing gum segments

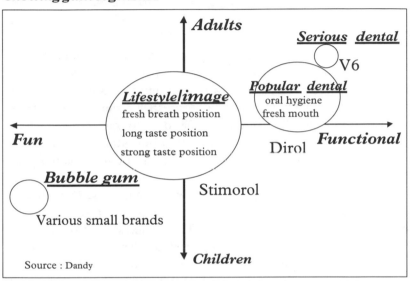

Note: The circles illustrate segment size. Dandy brands in each segment are shown.

The most common form of chewing-gum is the traditional American stick, but Dandy has specialized in dragées (coated tablets) and has a European market share of around 40% of the dragée segment and 20% overall. The total European market, including the CIS states (the former Soviet union), is estimated at 130,000 tons annually, worth approx. USD 1 billion, with the lifestyle segment accounting for 61% and the popular dental segment for 29%. Media spending continues to increase dramatically both in established and new markets. In some European markets, media spending on chewing-gum has nearly trebled over the past five years.

Though the annual chewing-gum consumption per capita in Europe (300g) is less than a third of the US figure, the market in Europe is not expected to grow rapidly. In the past decade, chewing-gum consumption in Western Europe has increased annually by 2-

3%. Dental and anti-smoking products are anticipated to grow more rapidly than the lifestyle segment.

The Dandy strategy

Adapting marketing activities to local situations in the post-war period has resulted in variations in product assortment, brand concept, design, prices and promotional parameters from country to country. There was a major change in the early 1990s after an eye-opening European consumer research project in 1989 revealed the power, international homogeneity and value of Stimorol. Vice-President of Finance, Ole Bielefeldt, stated: "We discovered that we owned an asset that was not in the books, with a value I should measure not in millions but probably in billions of Danish Kroner." The management group further discovered that Dandy's critical competence did not lie in the production of chewing-gum, but rather in the ability to create an image that could release an impulse buying reaction from a consumer.

Dandy decided to concentrate on Europe and closed its offices in the USA and Australia, a decision that was part of a strategy aimed at becoming big in small markets. The business-unit organization was created and European-wide committees were established to co-ordinate marketing activities. Sales & Marketing Vice-President Ove G. Rasmussen stated: " We wanted, and we are still in the process of creating, a professional marketing organization, but without losing the entrepreneurial spirit that is a hallmark of Dandy." Thus, Dandy's transformation has laid the foundation for evolution into a marketing-driven brand company.

Russia – land of opportunity

Dandy had already been doing business with government agencies in Eastern Europe for 15-20 years when the Soviet Union was dissolved in 1990. In that year, a new window of opportunity seemed to open up. CEO Lars Funder stated: "When we assessed the opportunities in Russia we came to an amazing and crucial discovery. There were 50 million color TV sets in Russia. Almost every household had a TV, though they might not have running water. The Communist Party had used television broadcasting to reach the people. But the best was yet to come. We could buy a 30-second national TV spot, which potentially could reach 100,000,000 people in the former CIS states, for about USD 500. A similar spot in the US would cost USD 250,000."

Steen Resen, Vice-President of Dandy Chewing Gum A/S, and responsible for the Russian market, stated: "Because TV spots were relatively cheap, we had the opportunity to support the brands properly. Fortunately, we were simultaneously being successful in Western Europe with a novelty product in the children's segment. In that way, Dandy Chewing Gum A/S generated the funds to support the Stimorol brand in Russia until sales suddenly went through the roof."

In 1992, Dandy made a contract with the Russian national television network to broadcast two advertising spots a day for six months. For three months thereafter, business remained limited to people who came in with plastic bags to Dandy's Moscow representative. But then people began arriving with old army trucks and wanted to buy the chewing-gum along with other western products. Some started to make money and Dandy began to send containers directly to bigger customers.

Following this initial success, Dandy increased advertising to five daily spots and bought the sponsorship for Russia's premier soccer league, which was renamed the Stimorol League. A local Dandy sales organization was set up in Russia in late 1993. By 1995, Stimorol was one of the best known brands in Russia, better known than Coca Cola or Marlboro. Sales in the CIS states grew from a few hundred tons in 1991 to almost 11,500 tons in 1995, 40% of Dandy's total sales volume. Dandy's market share in Russia currently exceeds 50%, and there are sales organizations in five of the CIS states.

The success factors

What are the critical factors behind the success in Russia? Lars Funder told us: "If you want to capitalize on an opportunity successfully, your basics, like production flexibility and delivery processes, have to be OK. Ours were. We had also initiated a marketing approach that was just what was needed in Russia. Finally, you need to understand how the local market works and adapt to that."

Ole Bielefeldt stated: "We made three important decisions. First of all, we maintained relatively high prices and a good profit margin.

Second, we did not give customer-friendly terms. In fact, in the beginning, small merchants paid cash and bigger clients had to pay in
advance before anything was shipped. In this way we had limited direct losses. But I believe the most important aspect was that we were
willing to take a risk by entering the Russian venture."

Lars Funder explains the change in strategy in the 1990s in the
following terms: "We used to think that if we were good at the main
production disciplines we would be able to make good products that
would be easy to sell. Now our belief is that we need to create the
demand and then adapt distribution and production accordingly."
In its move from a push to a pull strategy, Dandy increased marketing expenditures from 15% of turnover to 30%.

Strategy creation at Dandy

Dandy's activities are directed by a value-loaded company philosophy, stating that the company's aim is to give consumers a good
taste experience. The ultimate objective is "making people smile".
The company's long-term goals include being at least the number
two brand in their markets, and obtaining a 10% profit before tax on
sales.

There are a yearly business planning procedure and a hierarchical
business planning system. Group management specifies goals and
challenges for the coming year. These are then detailed in corporate
focus plans in main areas such as IT, human resources, production
and products. The business units make business-unit plans which
are further detailed by various sales companies in market business
plans and budgets. Finally, a link is made to departmental and personal objectives and goals for each employee. Longer-term opportunities and threats are scanned through both qualitative and quantitative scenarios intended to prioritize markets and identify lifestyle
trends.

All this could give the impression that Dandy is a very planned
company. It is not. Anders Bech, Human Resources Vice-President,
said: "Our decision process at Dandy is a two-tier system. We have
decisions which are made through a structured process, and decisions which are made outside all planning systems, based upon gut
feelings and intuition. This latter group of decisions often involves a
step-by-step experimental and learning approach."

Several Dandy managers highlight the value of learning in strategy creation. In Russia, Dandy has successfully captured the dental segment by introducing a new popular dental brand, Dirol. Experience in Russia has helped form a new strategy for the dental segment in Western Europe, a more popular positioning of the V6 brand.

Dandy favors taking calculated business risks in connection with new market opportunities, basing such decisions on a simple assessment of the opportunity and a quick calculation of potential revenues and costs. This is part of the Dandy culture.

Lessons learned

Dandy does not have the resources normally considered necessary to compete in brand wars. So why is Dandy a success? Some key principles can be highlighted:

Stay with the core business

Dandy has stayed with its core product, chewing-gum. This has kept the company focused on developing skills and technologies related to chewing-gum production, and has made it a world leader in dragée products. The company has also been firm on which markets to serve. If a decision is ever made to go outside Europe on a larger scale, it will probably be a very well-considered decision, though it will also be treated as a learning exercise.

Be able and prepared to change logic

It was a brand study in 1989 that triggered a new way of thinking. This led to a number of marketing changes, without which the Russian venture would probably not have been possible. The Russian experience fueled Dandy's transformation. The company was able to change logic for two main reasons:

- Key people do not seem stuck in functional responsibilities, and have a shared business and opportunity sense, making strategic changes based upon sound business facts easier to implement.
- The transformation to a marketing orientation, and later to being

a brand-driven company, was not a formalized strategy at the outset, which could have caused severe resistance. The strategy was formed during the learning process that began in the late 1970s, and which took off in the late 1980s and early 1990s.

Change through exploration and learning

At Dandy, there is a "yearly strategy process" which is used to determine goal-setting, strategy development, short-term action plans and budgets for activities in the year ahead. This process did not, however, trigger Dandy's transformation to a marketing-orientated, brand-driven company, and was not the cause of the move into the CIS states. These strategies emerged and matured with exploration and through learning.

Use strategic intuition and speed to grasp opportunities

There were no extensive feasibility studies in connection with the Russian opportunity. The critical factors were an ability to engage strategic intuition and to deliver speed in execution in order to benefit from the opportunity window before it closed. Dandy's experience is that, in a new market with an unknown environment, it is difficult to use formal planning because of the high number of unknown variables.

Experiment and learn

Dandy's informal, egalitarian structure, promotes new ideas in the international organization. In some areas, there is not much room for experiment, but when it comes to new markets and promotional campaigns, for example, Dandy learns by doing.

Keep the organization tuned

To manage growth like Dandy's, an organization needs to be well tuned. Dandy invests heavily in training and has created its own Stimorol Business School to train managers in new marketing thinking. The corporate culture, in which there is a "family" feeling, is also an important driving force, as are the challenges put forward by the management group, such as the total quality management project.

Adapt the business approach to the situation and the market

In Russia, Dandy adapted its organization and its market methods. Dandy believes it is critical to acquire the ability to develop a market using flexible applications of the various competencies needed at each stage.

Develop a sound business mentality

There are few text-book MBAs at Dandy. The company favors hands-on, entrepreneurial business people. It is not driven by ambitious goals or the need to satisfy shareholders, rather by the fun of doing business and exploring opportunities.

3.2 Politiken[1]
Towards a multimedia information center

Introduction

In 1993, Jens Carsten Nielsen was Vice-President of Sales & Marketing at Politiken, one of Denmark's largest newspaper groups. He could not see a profitable future in electronic media for newspapers, not even in the ventures his own company had entered. He felt that neither Politiken nor he had the necessary competencies. A year later, at the age of 49, he agreed to become president of the new division, Politiken Electronic Media. This case study will describe how Politiken assessed the developments and opportunities embodied in the "information revolution", and how the company has been developing its own direction in the world of electronic media, a technological and business transformation that will last into the next century.

Politiken's experience is interesting for three reasons. First, the move into electronic media is a major strategic shift for Politiken, in many ways completely different from the newspaper business which Politiken started in 1884. Second, the company has decided to go through a learning process rather than bring in new external people. Third, Politiken went into electronic services as far back as 1975, and thus already had a wealth of experience. Politiken's current turnover from electronic media is around 5% of what it derives from newspaper sales. Their goal of achieving 10% of newspaper revenues within 5 years is realistic, keeping in mind that the printed newspaper will not die for many years to come.

---

1. Casework completed in 1996

Politiken – history and main events

Politiken was established in 1884 by intellectuals opposed to the rul-ing classes and conservative government. It has remained the pre-ferred newspaper of trend-setting intellectuals. Its turnover is largely derived from subscription sales and advertisements.

A second newspaper within the group, Ekstra Bladet ("the extra newspaper"), was founded in 1904. It developed a very different style from Politiken. Ekstra Bladet is the *enfant terrible* of Danish newspapers. A popular tabloid, its revenue is based primarily on sin-gle-copy sales from news-stands.

In 1933, the Politiken group began book publishing, starting with fact-based year books, and later expanding its list to include Danish editions of international non-fiction best-sellers. The 1960s and the 1970s were a golden era for the Politiken group. Ekstra Bladet be-came Denmark's largest-selling newspaper in 1969, and Politiken the largest-selling morning newspaper in 1978.

The 1970s also saw the introduction of new information technol-ogy in production. The growing pains were as difficult for Politiken as for many other newspapers, with the typesetters – the group most affected – disrupting printing for long periods of time. The introduc-tion of information technology was the first step towards electronic media, leading to the birth of Polinfo, today a cornerstone of Politik-en's Electronic Media division. Polinfo is a news and information on-line database service, offering access to text archives and résumés of newspaper articles. When founded in 1975, it was the second such service in the world, beaten only by the New York Times.

From the mid-1980s, times were more difficult. Both Ekstra Bladet and Politiken lost circulation. Ekstra Bladet dropped from around 270,000 copies daily in 1977 to around 165,000 in 1995. Politiken's circulation fell from 155,000 in 1978 to 150,000 in 1995. Newspaper price increases did keep revenues stable. Howev-er, the launch of Denmark's first national commercial TV channel in 1987 had a dramatic negative effect on newspaper advertising rev-enues.

In the late 1980s and early 1990s, the Politiken group invested further in increasing efficiency and journalistic quality. But new ways of thinking and competing were needed. In 1994, therefore, Politiken introduced Politiken On Line, an electronic meeting place, and entered into a joint venture to publish and distribute CD-ROM titles. Also in 1994, to sharpen the focus and competitiveness of the group, Politiken was split into profit centers. Electronic media activities, including Polinfo, Politiken On Line, Polfoto (a press photography agency) and the CD-ROM business were placed under a separate division.

Organization, products and markets

Politiken is owned by a foundation, whose primary task is to secure the political and financial freedom of the group. Group equity was DKK 408 million (approximately USD 65 million) by the end of 1995. The chart below shows the group's main profit centers, excluding subsidiaries engaged in activities such as book publishing. The chart also shows the main business areas of the Electronic Media Division.

The Politiken group - organization

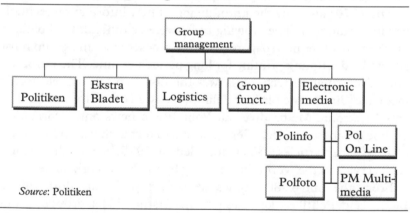

Source: Politiken

For the newspaper side of the business, the value-chain is almost fully integrated vertically, since Politiken is involved in everything from creating the newspaper's content to delivering the morning newspaper to subscribers. This is very different from the set-up in the electronic media business.

Polinfo makes résumés of, and indexes articles from, the newspapers in the Politiken group, and other major Danish newspapers. Services also include editorial materials from international news providers, such as the Financial Times and Reuters. Subscribers to

Polinfo are businesses, libraries and government agencies. Polinfo is Denmark's biggest database news service and employs 11 journalists. It is growing at a rate of 30% a year, measured in terms customer usage.

Polfoto, the in-house photo agency, also serves other Danish newspapers, magazines, and advertising agencies etc. Investment has been made in digital techniques for storing and transmitting pictures.

Politiken On Line is a subscription-based service. At a cost of about USD 10 a month, subscribers have access to an electronic meeting-place, a range of conferences discussing topics ranging from politics to exotic birds. Politiken On Line has 8,000 subscribers and is the biggest on-line meeting place for Danes. The concept of Politiken On Line is different from that of on-line services in the USA like America On-line, since Politiken produces very little content for it.

The Politiken group is still primarily a newspaper business. About 5% of total revenue comes from Electronic Media, and 5% from books and other publishing. The trend in group turnover and profits is shown below. In USD terms the turnover was approximately 230 million in 1995

Key figures - Politiken group

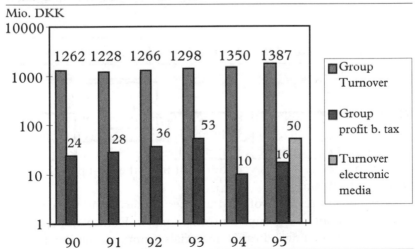

Source: Politiken

The Danish electronic media market

PC-based on-line services, the main part of Politiken's electronic media business is estimated by Politiken to have a yearly turnover in Denmark of DKK 500 million (approximately USD 80 million). The professional segment, specialized real-time services like Reuters financial services, news agency services, and news and information retrieval services like Polinfo, accounts for by far the larger part of turnover. The consumer segment, which includes Politiken On Line, is very small.

The capacity to accept multimedia services is often based on an index weighing the penetration of phone lines, TVs and personal computers. In such surveys, Denmark frequently ranks second (surpassed only by the USA) or perhaps third in the world. Politiken estimates that 37% of Danish households have PCs (15% with a modem connection). Although these figures should be interpreted cautiously, they suggest that Denmark has a solid foundation for the development of electronic media services.

The electronic media industry infrastructure

In developing its strategy for Electronic Media, Politiken has had to evaluate the value-chain. This has served as a basis for deciding the role Politiken should play. The chart below shows a simplified view of the value chain.

A simplified view of the electronic media value chain

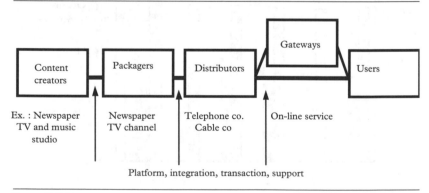

Source: Politiken

Jens Carsten Nielsen stated: "It is clear to us that we cannot control all elements in the value-chain like we do for newspapers. We will not be in the distribution business. The 'product' that flows through the value chain is data, so we have spent quite some time discussing elements like software platforms, integration and transactions between the various elements in the chain. These are the real future challenges. There are two elements which we have discussed in particular. The first is whether we should invest in server platforms to be used with the distribution networks provided by TeleDanmark (the Danish telephone company). The second is how to handle customer transactions, like billing."

The vision of the information factory

For Ejvind Sandal, CEO of the Politiken group one of the inspirations for the new vision was an analysis of the drawbacks of newspapers. "The problem with newspapers," he said, "is that we kill them every day, we lack space and they are expensive to distribute. With the help of electronics we can prolong the life of our information and re-use it, we can get all the space we want and we can distribute it cheaply."

Re-using information is central to the Politiken vision of a "multimedia information center" or, in more popular terms, "information factory". The idea is to make editorial data – text and pictures – independent, by collecting, organizing and storing them in common databases, from which they can be retrieved and tailored to a particular requirement. For example, a famous chef might write three recipes for a given Sunday issue of Politiken. These would then be made uniform, stored and indexed, and may later be used in the daily on-line shopping list, or even a book of exotic recipes.

Another important part of the Politiken vision is to strengthen information, not news. "We are in the information providing business, not the news providing business," explains Ejvind Sandal. "This is true of our on-line services as well. The purpose of information providing is to explain why, not to break the news." He explained this with the following flow chart.

One of Politiken's core competencies, and one that Polinfo shares, is the ability to provide an overview and a deeper understanding of the news. As stated by Thøger Seidenfaden, Editor-In-

A newspaper's strategic space

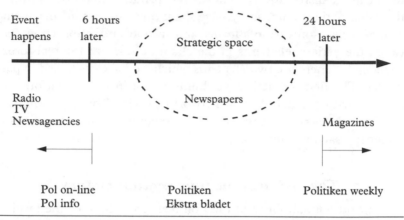

Source: Politiken

Chief of Politiken: "We are not afraid of competition from TV. Television can entertain and provoke emotions, but it also cuts up reality into small pieces, and serves it without connection or explanation...We must ensure that the newspaper does what it is best at, which is to provide an overview and the links that enable the reader to go into detail with what is both near and far away." *(Extract from "Velkommen I Politiken", an introduction to new subscribers)*

Another of Politiken's competencies is the ability to create brand loyalty. This competence has been passed on to Politiken On Line, which for newspapers is a gateway to the consumer, just like a retail shop.

The few specific guidelines for the Electronic Media Division are:

* use Polinfo and Polfoto as a foundation
* initially focus on business customers
* supplement the newspapers
* make money.

The last of these is important. This new division is expected to make money quickly, but a balance must be maintained. If too much emphasis is placed on making too much money too quickly, it may not develop properly. By the same token, if too much development is undertaken too soon, this could interfere with its ability to make money.

How the vision emerged

The decision to pay more attention to electronic media has been driven by two factors, according to Jens Carsten Nielsen. First, there were the difficulties apparent in the traditional newspaper business: "It was very clear to me that the newspaper industry as a whole had peaked in 1985, if you looked at a key figure like newspaper turnover. What really worried me as well was that I could see a drop in reading frequency among younger people (15-25 years). It was about a third of the figure for the population as a whole."

The second crucial element was Jens Carsten Nielsen's ad hoc discussions with people interested in electronic media. The editors of Polinfo and Politiken On Line had been very persistent in their promotion of the opportunities available in electronic media. They were among the first to understand the implications and potential of the "information revolution", and understood how to begin exploiting opportunities.

The decision to put so much effort into electronic media had to be approved by the board. Jens Carsten Nielsen remembered his first presentation to the board: "When I made the first presentation of our thoughts to the board, nobody seemed to understand. Like everybody else, they were thinking 'newspaper', and did not understand why I was talking about modems, the net, user interfaces and things like that. It was very much due to the strong support of Ejvind (Sandal), that we finally got board approval."

Two other aspects seem to be crucial in making decisions concerning electronic media, which were the commercial value of the activities and an openness to experimentation.

Experimentation

The corporate culture of Politiken is one of creativity, setting trends and being critical of conformity. Politiken has been a front-runner in many areas, as has Politiken On Line. But there have also been less successful ventures, though these were a natural consequence of experimentation. Politiken entered Diatel, a Danish version of the French Minitel that included financial transactions. However, in

1994 it was realized that this venture would probably never become a new Minitel, because of the growth of the Internet. Nevertheless, valuable contacts and alliances had been made.

The transformation

Politiken is in the early stages of transformation from a traditional, journalist-driven newspaper to a customer-driven information service. How big is this strategic change? The chart below indicates some of the differences between the newspaper business and the business of being a news provider based on on-line media.

Newspapers and on-line media – some differences

	Newspaper	**Electronic paper**
Life cycle stage	Past mature	Infancy
Product	One standard product	Customer forms product
Customer relationship	One-way communication	Dialogue
Nature of product	Text, pictures, graphics	Sound,text,video,graphics
News delay	Minimum 6 hours	None necessarily
Production	Rules, tradition	Learning by doing
Distribution	Rising costs	Falling costs
The physical product	Movable	Semi movable

Source: Politiken

Though the differences highlighted in the above chart might seem radical, Ejvind Sandal has another view of these changes: "Our strategy has not really changed. We are still focusing on the same target groups, and we still want to provide the same value. We still want to provide overview and background, it is just that the way we provide it will change"

Politiken's transformational challenge is in some ways parallel to the technological change the company went through in the 1970s. The concept of an "information factory" will change the organizational structure, journalistic tasks and work flow. Eventually it may change the power structure of the traditional company.

Over time, work processes and habits will change dramatically for all employees. Ejvind Sandal argued: "Today our newspaper people work in a day to day rhythm – one newspaper per day. When we move to providing on-line information, we will have to work in a continuous rhythm where the 'paper' is updated constantly "

Lessons learned – success factors
Changing business mission – technology does matter

Define the business you are in according to the basic needs you serve, say business strategists. Thus, the business mission for a stage-coach was transportation, while Politiken has defined its mission as "information providing", independent of technology or format. But just as employees in the stage-coach business might have loved horses, those at Politiken love newspapers, though not necessarily "on-line papers". Employees from the Electronic Media Division feel this sentiment this every day when they try to co-operate with the newspaper people, who are not really motivated to co-operate.

Can such an organization gradually transform into another kind of business, or should they start completely from scratch with new people? So far, Politiken has decided that the Electronic Media Division should stay close to the newspaper business, to act as an agent of change.

The concept of business "gardening"

Politiken has provided room for its employees to track down opportunities on a small scale. This process could be compared to gardening. When a "plant" is small, responsibility rests in the hands of the employees concerned. This approach has enabled the group to develop a unique opportunity, like Politiken On Line. Small investments have also been made in new businesses. In the case of Diatel, the amount invested was only 5%, but that was still enough to gain insight and learn.

Taking these businesses to the next step is a challenge. As a project grows, a more formalized/structured approach becomes necessary. This involves focusing on the concept in terms of services, customers and prices, large-scale investment and the development of marketing strategies. Politiken has decided to develop the electronic businesses within a single division, in order to create intellectual synergy between those people who are interested in electronic media. How business synergy should be established is not yet clear.

Protecting the present revenue stream

Politiken's strategic thinking is very much based on protecting existing revenues, thus providing the same basic value using new formats. Evidence of this thinking is provided by the decision not to
join the crowd who have been providing a free Internet paper and by
efforts to increase customer loyalty through Politiken On Line. It is
also interesting to note that Politiken considers the core competencies it will need in the future to be the same ones it needs today.
Rather than having a big competence-acquisition agenda, it prefers
to make alliances in order to gain access to new knowledge.

Think about value as well as technology

Technology issues often take up a good portion of management's
time, and the Politiken electronic division is no exception. Nevertheless, Politiken Electronic Media does manage to keep a watchful
eye on the value it provides to customers. This may be because the
managers have a journalistic and marketing background, not a tech-
nical one.

You can operate without a detailed three-year plan

Politiken does not have a detailed three-year, or even one-year plan
for its activities. The electronic media business is driven by a broad
sense of direction, which can change. The people at Politiken Electronic Media often feel they have come to a strategic cross-roads
where a fundamental decision on direction must be made. The vision has thus far remained clear, but only the first stepping stones
have been laid.

3.3 Infogrames[1]
Interactive business development

Introduction

The French company Infogrames produces entertainment software games for CD-ROM, SEGA and Nintendo consoles etc. These games are produced kind of like films, but since the game player decides how the "film" is to evolve, the game creator may have to produce a total playing time of 70 hours.

This is the story of a company founded by five young men who just wanted to start a company. They founded Infogrames and it grew fast – too fast. The company lost a lot of money, and nearly its life. The founders said they thereby learned a basic lesson in strategy. They survived the crisis, consolidated the company, and it is now growing rapidly again in terms of turnover and profits.

Infogrames' experience is interesting because the company has learned certain basic lessons on how to make money in a fast-growing market. In recent years, the drive to capitalize on entrepreneurial opportunity has been combined with sound strategic thinking, a mix which is often difficult to optimize.

The entrepreneurial history of Infogrames

The history of Infogrames can be divided into 4 phases:

1. Establishment and growth (1983-1986)
2. Crisis and fight for survival (1987-1991)
3. New strategy and growth (1992-1995)
4. Diversification (1996 –)

1. Casework completed in 1996

Infogrames - key figures

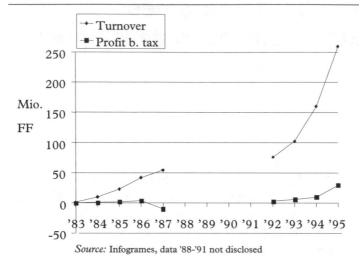

Source: Infogrames, data '88-'91 not disclosed

1. Establishment and growth (1983-1986)

Among the five young men who founded Infogrames were engineers who saw software development opportunities for the new computers being introduced in French schools. This led to Infogrames being awarded contracts to develop tutorial games. In 1986, Infogrames started another line of business, which was the development of inter-active programs based on premium telephone charges for networks like the French Minitel. This was another growth market.

Infogrames was then growing very fast, driven by the founders' enthusiasm and an understanding of inter-activity developed during the first school projects. Thomas Schmider, one of the founders, said: "The organization was driven by fun. Everybody was very ex-cited about interactive games. We almost did not have to pay people to work here. They did it because they thought it was fun."

2. Crisis and consolidation (1987-1991)

By 1987, Infogrames had grown into a group of 27 companies, with activities ranging from developing technologies in co-operation with MIT to publishing computer magazines and advertising through a wholly-owned agency. The group was, however, still small, with a turnover of around FFR 50 million (approximately USD 8.5 million). Infogrames had also invested heavily in the games business. Resources had to be put into basic technology development and the market was still rather small. Costs exploded at Infogrames and a distributor went bankrupt. Infogrames suffered a loss of FFR 10 million in 1987, and had a FFR 24 million overdraft. They were now in crisis.

The founders concluded that the vision and inspiration of Infogrames "to be like the Walt Disney of inter-activity" was still valid, but the way business was be conducted had to be much more efficient and selective. Thomas Schmider said Infogrames had learned five basic lessons:

"1. You have to understand the *real* market. In an emerging market like interactive games, there is no one technology standard. There may be 22 million machines world-wide today with CD-ROM drives, but maybe only a quarter of them have the technological ability to use our games;

2. You have to balance your product portfolio. A software game has a life-cycle, and you need to balance the life cycles of your portfolio of games in order to balance your cash flow;

3. You have to focus on certain activities. We wanted to control the game value-chain from idea to customer, and we still want that. However, we have abandoned basic technology development, and now we even outsource certain parts of game development;

4. Focus on the keys to profit, which in our case means controlling development costs, securing quick market penetration, and ensuring a long market life for a game;

5. You have to let management focus on core values. One of our initial success factors was our ability to inspire employees by using a person-to-person leadership style. We lost this somewhat during the periods of growth and crisis. Now we have regained it and have begun to focus on transferring it to all managers."

Infogrames developed these principles between 1989 and 1991, and began aligning the company to conform to them.

3. New strategy and growth (1992-1995)

Infogrames' business was now defined as the *production* and *distribution* of interactive home entertainment for all types of media. Relationships with the fast-growing game companies Nintendo and

SEGA began adding significantly to Infogrames' own growth. The narrower focus on critical activities and better project management also began having a positive effect on operating profits.

In 1993, outside investors (including the Pathé media group) were brought in to strengthen the financial foundation, and to develop business alliances. The company was listed on the small-company stock exchange in Paris in that same year. In 1994, Infogrames began work on a major new initiative. It was clear to the company that off-line games would gradually be replaced by on-line games, e.g. someone in Paris playing in real time with someone in Nice. With the backing of new outside investors, Infogrames started to develop Infonie, a telephone line based on-line medium for interactive games and other services.

4. Diversification (from 1996)

The Infonie concept has been developed into a complete on-line service, including shopping, news and practical information. It is not Internet-based, but provides access to the Internet. Infonie is viewed by Infogrames as a multimedia (text, video, sound and pictures) version of the Minitel.

Infonie, now incorporated in a company controlled by Infogrammes listed on the Paris stock exchange, is a *distribution* activity, with a network of servers all over France, and is thus very different from the off-line interactive games. These distribution activities, estimated to have required in all an investment of FFR 200 million (approximately USD 35 million), have been in operation since early 1996.

Why does Infogrames want to create its own network rather than use the Internet? Thomas Schmider: " Infonie is a big gamble for us, but we are sharing the risk with others. We view the Internet as a fantastic global communication network, but it does not provide the sound, video, graphics or inter-activity we need for our games. I believe that people will choose special channels for special purposes, just like with TV channels."

Today more than 50% of Infogrames turnover is from outside France. Infogrames has sales companies in Belgium, Great Britain, Germany and Spain. Interactive entertainment accounts for about 75% of group turnover, while Minitel and similar services (including Infonie) account for only about 25%.

Game development and marketing

Game development is Infogrames' most critical process. As with films, overall responsibility is in the hands of an executive producer. A given project may involve as many as 80 people, 25 man-years, and direct costs of FFR 10 million. To all this must be added manufacturing and marketing expenses, bringing total costs up to FFR 20 million (approximately USD 3.5 million). Program testing, including consumer testing, is done in-house and is a major component of these high quality Infogrames games.

The Infogrames publishing team turns programs into commercial products, organizing packaging design, translation to other languages, and user instructions etc. Manufacture of a game and physical accessories like the box are outsourced. International marketing, promotion and sales are through sales companies and distributors. The overall process requires a combination of skills which would normally be divided into two separate businesses. Olivier Goulay, an Infogrames producer, explained: "We produce the way movies are produced, but we publish the way books are published."

At Infogrames, they have learned that projects should not all be treated equally, going through the same process or value-chain. Thomas Schmider said: "We have always considered the idea behind the game and the ability to make it interactive as essential. This continues to be true, though we have learned that it is equally important to apply different business models to different types of projects. In a project based on any new technology, certain kinds of skills are critical. In a project based on a mature technology, other types of skills are needed."

Strategy as an understanding of value and cost

The lessons Infogrames learned during the crisis years are part of their business thinking today. During the company's managed growth process after the crisis years, a primary strategy has been to focus on the value and cost of what the company is doing or wants to do. This strategy is based on creating products that provide superior entertainment and education experiences. The company's learning abilities and skills in this area have been developed to include an understanding of critical elements in the different game and educational market segments.

Understanding value is also a question of putting only those elements into a program that add more value than they cost to develop. One critical factor is to understand the extent of the value opportunity of a game and the passion it creates. Thomas Schmider explains what Infogrames has learned from studying the movie industry: "We view our games the same way Disney views their movies. We sell intellectual rights. Our games are not just boxes, but products that can be leveraged to various hardware platforms, comic books and arcade machines. This extends the life-cycle of a product from the normal 6 months to 3-4 years."

Infogrames actually has to think globally. With total development costs of approx. FFR 10 million for a product before spending on marketing and distribution, break-even approaches minimum sales of 100,000 copies.

Organization and strategy creation

The Infogrames organization is very complex. The diagram below provides a simplified view:

The networked organization at Infogrames

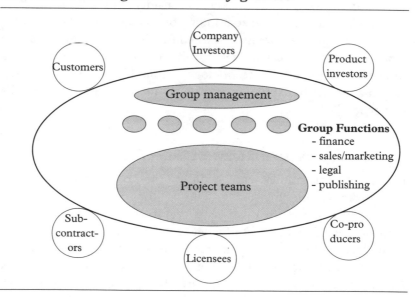

Source: Infogrames

The organization is complex primarily because of the way in which Infogrames products are developed and distributed. Entertainment and educational programs are often developed in co-operation with publishers and investors, with cost-sharing and royalty agreements. Olivier Goulay: "The production of the CD-ROM on Napoleon involved museums, two publishers, one of our shareholders and an outside investor. It was like a joint venture."

Good project management is important to Infogrames, and attracting "interactive" talent is essential. Thomas Schmider stated: "When we started the company, we primarily attracted computer freaks. For them it was not just a job, and much was learned simply by doing. Now we offer a career, and our work is based on the skills and principles we ourselves teach new employees. We also have a trainee program each summer for 200-300 people"

However, even though Infogrames has moved into a phase in which everything is more organized, it is still the fun of working on the job that drives the employees. Thomas Schmider argues that his most important management task is to create an atmosphere in which employees can perform optimally. This probably does set limits on the size of the organization. Eric Coquaz, financial manager, stated: "We prefer to work in teams, and the management style we practice limits the number of people we can have in one physical organizational unit. We are 300 people now, and I think that is about the limit. The next thing will be to replicate our model in a new unit."

Lessons learned – success factors

How has Infogrames managed to grow fast and profitably in a difficult and constantly changing market? To address this question, we have highlighted three significant principles, listed below.

Interactive business development

Infogrames, although a small company, has been able to undertake very large projects, not alone, but in co-operation with others. A large part of Infogrames business is done as joint-ventures. This has proven to be a sound means for sharing risks and acquiring new learning skills. However, it does demand an ability to find the right partners and projects, a capacity to develop project concepts jointly with others, and excellent project-management skills and systems.

Visions that unite and motivate

Companies like Infogrames are driven by visions of opportunities, as well as the challenge of turning them into a reality. At Infogrames, there are a few key people who can create visions that employees, business partners and investors understand and find attractive. These shared visions knit the many people in the Infogrames networks together. They are without doubt a major motivational factor in the organization, pushing the limits of its capabilities, and optimizing performance.

Learning to take risks

At the outset, Infogrames engaged in a wide variety of activities, stretching the financial and managerial resources of the company, and putting it at risk. Infogrames still takes risks, but does so armed with the learning skills and experience gained from the crisis in the late 1980s. The economic and strategic desirability of the Infonie project, for example, has been carefully evaluated, with limits set on the financial risk, which has been isolated by incorporating the project into a new company with co-investors.

3.4 DRU [1]
Knowledge-based subcontracting

Introduction

The Dutch company Dru is a subcontractor in metal components, with an annual turnover of about USD 25 million. Dru went through difficult times in the 1980s and early 1990s, but is now in the middle of a remarkable turnaround under new management. Dru is a good example of how a company can find its way out of a difficult situation by focusing on its ability to learn, rather than just its products.

Company history

The history of Dru dates back to 1754, when it began as a metal-working business. They continue to work in this industry, though in the 1950s, they diversified into gas heaters. In the 1960s, Dru became one of the 30 biggest companies in Holland.

In 1972, the Dru group was taken over by Internatio Muller, a conglomerate. The company missed the gas central-heating wave in the mid-1970s and this side of the business began a gradual decline. At that time, sheet-metal activity was mainly dependent on large contracts with a fairly limited number of customers. Some of these major contracts became a problem, because Dru was unable to fulfill logistical requirements without substantial extra cost, causing this side of the business to become a major loss-maker.

In 1991, Dru was taken over by Wolter-Schaberg/Schuttersveld, a group specialized in turning round problem companies. Dru was split into three separate legal units, including Dru Industrial Products and Services, the subject of this case study.

1. Casework completed 1996

Dru – key figures 1991-1996

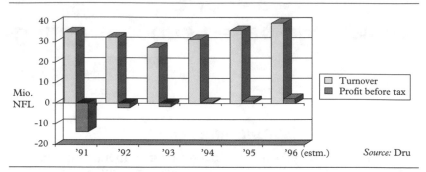

Source: Dru

The chart below shows Dru's performance over a recent six year period. It should be noted in comparison that, according to Dru, there are few sheet-metal businesses in Europe that are doing very well, actually achieving profits of 8-10% as a percentage of turnover. The majority, including Dru, average profits of 1-3 % of turnover.

The strategy behind the turnaround

In 1991, Dru was in severe crisis. CEO Hans Leliveld stated: "Dru was like a leaking ship. We decided not use pumps, but instead to plug the hole, sail the ship to the nearest harbor and perform a total repair." The Dru way of plugging that hole was tough. From one day to the next, there was a reduction in staff from 380 to 220. Then management began looking at Dru from a different perspective. The initial picture was not positive. There were expensive personnel, an old inefficient factory, few customers, price pressure from buyers, new competitors in Eastern Europe, and fluctuations in raw-material prices. But they discovered that there was one area in which Dru had a particular strength, which was their ability to produce sheet-metal components to very narrow tolerances.

This realization was the starting point of a change in strategy. Dru wanted to increase its customer base and started looking at product categories in which the company's special capability could be exploited, and where price was less of a competitive issue. Hans Leliveld said: "We were looking for profitable new customers to help us expand the business, but we were also looking for ways to reduce the power that customers had over us. We did this by focusing on the manufacture of specialty parts that few companies in the world like us could produce, as well as small volumes not attractive to Asian competitors." Thus, by 1995, Dru's customer base had grown to 20 companies, compared with six in the late 1980s.

Change to a product-based organization

Another need was to make the organization more efficient. There were problems with co-operation between sales and marketing, engineering and manufacturing. The Dru solution was to create business teams (order-processing teams) consisting of people from sales, engineering and production. There was also a changeover to product orientation in manufacturing (where most people are employed). There are now no team managers, and there is a high degree of decentralization in production. Today, Dru produces the same output as in 1990, but with 60% fewer personnel.

A new business mission

In recent years there has been an increase in outsourcing by big companies. Being one of these subcontractors, Dru has chosen to redefine its role. "Companies do not subcontract just because it is cheaper or more flexible," explains Hans Leliveld. "They also do it to gain access to skills that can make them more competitive. We do not just produce according to strict specifications, but are also asked to use our learning abilities to improve product designs in terms of both quality and cost." Thus, Dru now defines its business mission as helping its customers make more money, and offering support for their business strategies.

As Dru's business has improved, so has its view of its own capabilities. Hans Leliveld stated: "We are becoming a learning-based company. We sell manufacturing and product concepts. We know how to run an efficient sheet-metal business. We are able to copy this concept and set up new factories."

Strategy creation and lessons learned

The take-over by Wolter-Schaberg/Schuttersveld was not accompanied by huge capital injections. Nor was new management brought in from outside. The new owner's contribution was to assist Dru in systematically establishing a new perspective on the attractiveness of serving different customer and product segments.

Benefiting from a limited sales and marketing budget

A limited sales and marketing budget can be a positive force for change of attitudes. Hans Leliveld explains: "When we had a big sales budget, sales went down. When we cut the budget, we started focusing on selected individual sales." This narrower emphasis made sales people concentrate on obtaining and satisfying a single customer at a time, helping Dru to penetrate new segments. Assisted by Schuttersveld, Dru did its own market research. Lengthy interviews clearly established what the requirements of new customers were.

Your customers may be your best consultants

One of Dru's new customers is Kodak's medical equipment business. Dru has learned a lot from working with Kodak, where performance is measured on a scorecard related to areas critical to its success. Based on this scorecard, Kodak has defined tough goals for Dru. These demands have helped push through the shake-up at Dru, according to Hans Leliveld. Similar demands have also been made by other world-class customers that Dru has since acquired.

Stumble into opportunities with an open mind

You may not be able to see an opportunity that is staring you right in the face, though you can remedy this by putting on the right glasses. The initial contact with Kodak was established when the Dru sales manager was visiting the Kodak copier people and by chance met someone from the Kodak medical equipment business. They ended up discussing production solutions for certain metal frames. Five years earlier this sales manager might not even have been on the lookout for new customers, and even if he had met one, he might not have thought of her/him as such. He probably would have been narrowly focused on copier frames, not the capability of producing complicated sheet-metal components.

Learn to live with disappointment

Not everything has gone well for Dru during the past six years. There have been disappointments, including customers and suppliers who have offered little support. As a former speed-skating champion, Hans Leliveld compared the situation with his sport: "There is only one number one in each race, and you seldom win every time. There will be disappointments."

For Hans Leliveld, it is the process of creating a better company that is interesting. Returning to the speed-skating analogy, if you are only in the sport in order to compete in races, you will probably never become number one. You have to like the hard work between the races as well.

Hands-on management

Dru emphasizes the belief that effective hands-on management requires a maximum number of people in one organizational unit to be 250. With anything larger, the management style and slim overhead structure would need to change fundamentally.

3.5 Jansen Group[1]
Cutting (back) to survive

Introduction

In 1989, Auke Koops van't Jagd became Director of Purchasing at Jansen, a Dutch meat-processing business. This was a key position, since purchasing accounted for roughly 70% of turnover. In 1993, it became clear to Auke Koops van't Jagt that over-capacity in the industry was becoming a grave problem for the Jansen Group. Two years later, Auke Koops van't Jagd was appointed president of the Jansen Group, and a major transition ensued.

This is the story of how the Jansen Group re-focused its strategy and exploited the restructuring of the industry in a remarkable and continuing turnaround. In the process, turnover was cut by 1/3, but the group is again profitable. The challenges that the Jansen Group faced and still faces are not unusual for medium-sized, family-owned companies. In achieving its turnaround, the group has had to balance the interests of many stakeholders and use entrepreneurial business skills under great time pressure.

Company history

The Jansen Group was founded in 1952 by two brothers. The company's initial activity was the slaughtering of pigs and processing the meat. When the next generation took over in the 1980s, the group grew rapidly, acquiring a beef abattoir, a bacon factory, a bigger pork processing company, and a fat-rendering plant. By the beginning of the 1990s, the Jansen Group had a turnover of HFL 600m (approximately USD 350 million), nearly 600 employees, and was among the top six Dutch meat-processing businesses. It was at this time that the severity of the industry's problems began to show.

---

1. Casework completed 1996

In the early 1990s, most Dutch abattoirs were losing money because of heavy over-capacity. The government and industry associations formed a group to solve the problem. This group's work was based on a solidarity strategy, whereby abattoirs that choose not to close were to pay compensation out of their own future revenues to those that did. But the group was never able to agree on a solution, even after five years of negotiations.

Another problem was that many meat-processing companies were in the bulk business, adding very little value and leaving the fine cutting and preparation of meat to retail chains and butchers. Oversupply and increasing competition in bulk meat from abroad put severe pressure on prices. The abattoirs and meat-processing companies were caught in a profit trap. The prices at which pigs were bought were centrally fixed by a farmer's board, and selling prices were difficult to maneuver because over-supply put power into the hands of the retail chains. On top of this, the cash-flow situation was difficult because suppliers had to be paid in advance, while customers typically enjoyed one or two months' credit.

By the end of 1994, the Jansen Group was in major difficulty, having posted a heavy loss in the last quarter of the year. The group's bankers were worried. Something had to be done. Then on 1 January 1995, at the bank's recommendation, Auke Koops van't Jagd became CEO.

Transforming the Jansen Group

Auke Koops van't Jagd remembers that his initial thought when appointed CEO was: "We are doing something completely wrong. This is not merely a question of doing what we already do a little better." He began an analysis of the company's internal and external problems, identifying four main needs:

1. Reduction of the unprofitable slaughtering business;
2. Demonstration of leadership;
3. Development of more profitable value-adding activities;
4. Changing production/volume thinking.

He had to prioritize his actions, and began by focusing on the first two challenges: "We had to show our stakeholders, primarily our bank, that we could manage this situation. We needed to show that we could take and implement the tough decisions." Thus, in early 1995, the Jansen Group acted, and contributed to the restructuring of the entire industry by agreeing to close two abattoirs, which resulted in receiving payment for the closure of unprofitable businesses. In addition, in a rather creative business move, the company sold one of the sites to the local municipality, which for quite some time had wanted the abattoir shut down for environmental reasons. Auke Koops van't Jagd explained: "We made some pretty big and fast decisions in our restructuring phase. They were all based on simple but sound calculations and the will to see opportunities where others saw only problems and threats."

The chart below shows the trend in the Jansen Group 's turnover, and profits during the years of crisis and turnaround. The chart, however, does not reveal the full extent of the problems faced in 1994 and 1995. The extraordinary income causes these years to appear better than they actually were. The Jansen Group is on schedule for its best profit in five years on a turnover that is more than one-third less than in the previous years – approximately USD 225 million.

Jansen Group: key figures 1992-96

	1992	1993	1994	1995	1996 (est.)
Turn-over	640	629	614	600	400
Profit before tax	4.5	2.5	1.0	-3.0	5.0

Source: Jansen Group   All figures in Hfl. millions

Auke Koops van't Jagd said that the restructuring at the Jansen Group was not a democratic process. With the bank's support, he used the crisis to put the organization through a painful transformation process. "I made it clear to all employees", he stated, "that we were fighting for survival, and used this to make deeper cuts in the organization than would normally have been possible. But I made sure it did not get out of hand, and that I had the backing of the key people in the organization, including the owners."

A strategy for future growth

It was clear to Auke Koops van't Jagd that the way out of the profit trap was to add more value to the meat. There needed to be a gradual withdrawal from the bulk market, because the company did not have the size to obtain economies of scale or negotiating advantages. He used this diagram to explain the long-term plan:

The value-adding activities

Strategic tasks – Jansen group

Slaughter	
First cuts	focus on cost-efficiency
Main parts	
Special cuts	develop/fine tune
Packaging	
Cooked/ready-made	prepare/create strategic partnerships
Consumer	

Source : The Jansen Group

The Jansen Group has continued emphasizing cost-efficiency in the initial links of the value chain, but innovatively. One possibility has been to transfer acquired learning skills and meat-cutting to abattoirs in Eastern Europe, where costs are dramatically lower.

Adding more value has meant preparing end-user cuts and packaging for supermarket chains that do not have their own facilities. It may also mean taking over the butchery departments of retail chains that wish to focus on their own core competencies in selling and distribution. Eventually, it may also involve preparing complete ready-to-cook meals.

This strategy represents a complete change of thinking. Auke Koops van't Jagd stated: "We have to understand the business of the customer if we are to deliver added value. We have to stop thinking only about the number of pigs we process. " The Jansen Group has also become aware that this new strategy requires new skills, especially in logistics. For example, supermarkets may want just-in-time delivery twice a day, direct to the meat counter.

Lessons learned and strategy creation

Seeing the opportunities embodied in threats

The Jansen Group turned the unpleasant situation of over-capacity and industry restructuring into an opportunity to close down, at low cost, operations which were not profitable. Management benefited from making the effort to evaluate an option that on the surface did not look attractive, but then suddenly became so. Two deals were thus knitted together – payment for closing down and payment for selling the site.

Learning from early failures

Auke Koops van't Jagd is from a farmer family with 10 children. He experienced his father's uphill and eventually unsuccessful battle. This experience helped him in determining a new direction for the Jansen Group, to concentrate on providing value, not volume. Had the Jansen Group stayed on the old course, the uphill battle would have been just a waste of resources because the company would have eventually died anyway. The old strategy was no longer viable, because times had changed.

Making sound business calculations

The Jansen Group has benefited greatly from its ability to make quick, sound business calculations based on plausible assumptions. The bank has apparently recognized this as proof of a good understanding of the economics of the business. This has added to the credibility of both short and long-term plans.

Do not seek advice from too many others

In the formation of this new strategy and transformation of the company, the new group CEO has been relatively alone in the decision-making process. Auke Koops van't Jagd does not believe you should ask too many "experts" for directions when you are facing opportunities and/or threats. He says that leads to confusion, and that learning and experimenting on your own is much more valuable.

Balancing interests and purposes

When a company is in major transition, it is of critical importance to be able to strike a balance between short-term and long-term considerations, and to balance as much as possible the interests of the various stakeholders. For the Jansen Group, presentation of a reliable short-term cost-cutting plan in combination with the new strategy of adding value was crucial to obtaining bank financing.

Part Four

**How five companies
changed strategic direction**

4.1 Introduction

This chapter concludes on the experiences of five companies that changed strategic direction. They were selected for a number of reasons:

- All had undergone transformations and were achieving improved financial performance as a consequence;
- They all made creative use of opportunities or overcame size disadvantages;
- They represent different industries and a variety of ownership structures;
- Their change of direction followed a period of stagnation or even decline.

All are medium-sized, with turnovers ranging between USD 25 million and USD 325 million. In our view, however, the lessons they learned, as well as the conclusions drawn from their experiences in the final section of this report, are equally relevant to larger and smaller companies.

These case studies are derived from in-depth interviews with up to 10 people in each company, primarily at the senior management level, as well as background material supplied by the companies. Our questions were not based on preconceived ideas but designed to elicit an understanding of the companies, their history, their business activities and markets, and how they determined their direction and implemented their strategies.

4.2 The Five Companies

As can be seen in the chart below, the companies selected represent both consumer and industrial products, and services as well as manufacturing. Ownership structures vary widely, including family and senior-management ownership, foundation status, stock-exchange listing and ownership by a conglomerate. The organizational structures are also different, though as we shall see, there are certain common organizational principles. All except Politiken are very active internationally. While none are market leaders, each tries to achieve leadership in selected markets or product niches.

The five companies

Name	Nationality	Founded	Main business	Turnover ($m 1995)
DANDY	DK	1915	Chewing gum	255
Politiken	DK	1884	Newspapers	245
Infogrames	F	1983	Entertainment software	55
Dru	NL	1754	Sheet metal	25
Jansen Group	NL	1952	Meat processing	325

The chart below summarizes changes that occurred, and company performance thereafter. Change began as late as 1995 for one company, and as early as the late 1980s for another.

Each company underwent fairly radical changes in their beliefs about what leads to success (business logic), but none of them did so by hiring new management. In three of the five companies, change was led by a new CEO, but these people had been promoted from within. The impetus of change was serious financial difficulty (Dru, Jansen Group, Infogrames), and/or market- or technology-driven opportunity (Dandy, Politiken, Infogrames). In all cases, the need for change is traceable back to changes in the external company environments.

Change at the five companies

Company	Change	Performance thereafter
DANDY	From production to brand-driven Penetrated new markets (the CIS)	Turnover : x 2 Profit : x 3
Politiken	Established a new electronic media business	New business (turnover $10m)
Infogrames	From unfocused growth to controlled, focused hyper growth	Turnover : x 4 From loss to profit
Dru	Restructuring and focused development of key capability	Consolidated turnover, back to profits
Jansen Group	Restructuring and focus on adding value	Reduced turnover by 33%, Return to profit

The improvements in performance cannot be explained solely by change in direction. With two of the companies, the need for efficiency was also instrumental. But various factors suggest that change in direction was indeed a major factor.

4.3 What drives a change in direction?

It could perhaps be assumed that major changes in direction are the result of complex processes of evaluation, during which insightful visions are discussed, markets and capabilities are thoroughly analyzed, and alternative strategies are assessed – what could typically be labeled "strategic planning". In the companies we studied, this was not the case. Although four of the companies regularly practiced some form of strategic planning, the change in direction originated from events initiated outside the planning process. (One of the "planning" companies is currently even questioning the value of its fairly complex planning system.)

Opportunity is a key factor

For these companies, strategic change was triggered by the pursuit of de facto opportunities, as well as the experiences and learning such opportunities generated. Politiken's "Politiken On Line" service, for example, was a completely new way of interacting with the newspaper's readers, and the experience of operating the service led the way toward establishing the new Electronic Media Division.

Why then is the planning process not helpful to opportunity-based strategic change? Our case studies suggest the following reasons:

- It cannot be known *when* an opportunity will arise;
- It cannot be known *how* an opportunity will arise;
- Implementation of a response to an opportunity is non-linear;
- Planning and administration slow down implementation drastically;
- The outcome is uncertain (the "net present value" concept, NPV, is difficult to apply.)

The "opportunity approach" is refreshingly simple and straightforward. It does not require extensive market studies, big investment programs, or detailed analyses of competitor activity.

The case study companies have adopted a learn-by-doing, step-by-step approach to business development, clearly placing value on speed when capitalizing on opportunities, as well as limiting risk. There also appears to be a general consensus that opportunities and threats do not appear in any preferred manner, or even when they might be convenient and wanted. They must be seized upon when they occur.

Thus, applying basic business-development or entrepreneurial principles seems to be far more important than planning as a catalyst for strategic change. It is also worth noting that a single opportunity can carry enormous importance. At Dandy, pursuing one opportunity resulted in business that now contributes to roughly 40% of business volume, and even more in terms of profits.

Strategic thinking helps maintain focus

This is not to say that the companies studied do not use strategic thinking or principles in their business development. Indeed, Infogrames learned the hard way the consequences of a lack of strategic thinking, which was just how dangerous it can be to attempt exploiting opportunities in an uncontrolled and unfocused way. At Infogrames, certain strategy frameworks now help the company to more narrowly focus its business activities both horizontally and vertically. In some of the other companies, strategic planning has been useful in optimizing their bread-and-butter activities. It also seems that strategy tools have been helpful during periods of consolidation, following opportunity-driven periods of expansion.

Strategic thinking seems to be very important to any action program in pursuit of an opportunity. Throughout the implementation process, management is typically confronted with fundamental strategic questions. With Dandy's Russian venture, those responsible have had to make one major decision after the other, e.g. form of distribution, product adaptation, organization and pricing. These strategic decisions were made on the basis of an understanding of local conditions. Typical text book strategies could offer little help, and the mechanisms of the Russian market had very little in common with those in other Dandy markets.

Although the application of rigid strategic planning or budgeting procedures to uncertain opportunities seems fruitless, some of the companies were under pressure to do this from key stakeholders – the board or bank, for example. While a strategic or business plan provides a kind of control for a business development project, if this project is related to an uncertain opportunity, the sense of control is false.

Vision is an instrument of change

Vision appears to have been an important instrument of change in each of these companies, and not merely in the typical usage of what a company should look like 10 years from now. The use of vision in these companies was much simpler and more specific, and because of this, perhaps much more demanding as well. The key ability they have all demonstrated is envisioning specific business opportunities in light of, for example, changing technologies and markets. Such vision builds on specific, often mind-opening insights and strong beliefs about business potential, as well as on ways of fulfilling that potential.

Several of the companies utilize analogy, not only to assist in creating a vision, but also to make the vision attractive to employees. For example, Infogrames compared itself with companies in the film industry to explain its business vision. Some of the five companies also use the traditional, rather grand and less specific 'vision of the future'. Nevertheless, a "think big, but take small steps" philosophy best describes the thinking in those companies.

These companies developed their visions and formed their opinions on the basis of experience, intuition and data. However, data in the form of predictions for specific market size seem to play a minor role, because opportunities often relate to areas which are difficult to analyze. It is, for example, difficult to predict how big the market for on-line services could be in 10 years. One estimate is as good as the next.

Contradicting existing business logic

Our observations suggest that a change in direction can be fueled by the pursuit of opportunities which contradict existing business logic. A business logic is a company's perception of what it should be doing and how it should be doing it in order to become successful. Having developed such a logic, if accurately defined and effectively implemented, may be advantageous during stable times. But if it does not change when the business environment changes, it often becomes a constraint. In all five companies studied, the pursuit of opportunities was to some degree influenced either by a series of events or by a single "aha!" experience that effectively challenged or contradicted the existing logic.

At Dandy, a study showing the surprisingly high value of Dandy brands contradicted the established way of thinking, and demonstrated very effectively that the Dandy core capability was to create brand value. This promoted a change in approach that was of great significance to the Russian venture. At the Jansen Group, a financial crisis convinced the organization that it was doing something completely wrong, and that it was essential to develop new, more profitable business opportunities.

You do not need to stretch goals

This statement is in contrast to the popularly held belief that it is important to push goals or scorecarding to their limits. In each of these companies, management had probably made commitments to the board and other stakeholders regarding quantitative financial goals. But such quantitative goals do not appear to have been used as guidelines within the organization. One explanation may be that, when changing direction and moving into unknown territory, it is much more difficult to quantify ambitions. It would be difficult for Politiken, as an example, to predict how big its electronic media business might be in two years, and impossible to forecast five years into the future.

So how can companies attempt to control progress? One way would be to compare actual progress to a given vision. Another would be to control short term pay-off. This differs from the practice of certain larger companies, which may accept several years without profits during new ventures. The companies in our case study seem to have emphasized achieving very short-term pay-back. An explanation for this may be that, with a large company, profits really begin to roll in once sales move into a mass-market phase. For smaller players, however, there is perhaps a higher degree of uncertainty about achieving such sales volumes.

Direction evolves from a patchwork of decisions

Only one of the five companies referred to a business plan or strategic plan as encompassing the direction of the company. For the other companies, direction seemed to be derived from a patchwork, including concept papers, presentations, scenarios and ideas in the minds of key people. This indicates that their directions have changed as opportunities evolved.

Though change itself remains a constant factor in some of these companies, there are also elements of stability. Infogrames has established fairly consistent principles for games development, just as Dandy has instituted certain well-defined processes for the development of TV commercials. It is the ability to simultaneously optimize effectiveness (what you do) and efficiency (how you do it) that matters.

Avoidance of intense competition

It is interesting to note that, in several of the companies, opportunity thinking was very much influenced by a defensive business philosophy. They were concerned with protecting their existing revenue streams, and they sought opportunities where competition was limited, such as in niches. They also thought more in terms of creating new value rather than trying to obtain a bigger slice of an established market. They seemed to have favored business environments in which they were the sole or dominant supplier, Dandy in Russia being a case in point.

4.4 The business development process

Four of the five case companies would not consider being driven by innovation, as for instance the US company 3M is. Nevertheless, they have all developed ideas and/or opportunities that have fueled changes in strategic direction. This makes it of great interest to look at some of the features found common among their methods for developing business opportunities. Thus, in this section, we shall attempt to analyze the business development processes these five companies have gone through, as well as what appears to have been the critical success factors in these processes.

The business development process

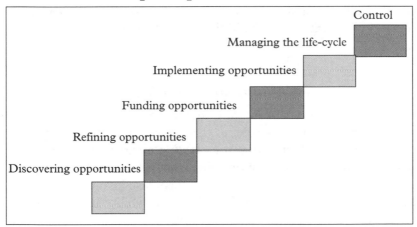

Discovering opportunities

Discovery of opportunities is very much linked to people. Two people from different companies with different backgrounds looking at the same market might not see the same opportunities. In our study cases, opportunities were discovered in various ways:

a) Through an understanding of new technologies;
b) Through customer/market interaction;
c) Through seeing an opportunity hidden inside a problem;
d) Through a better understanding of self-capabilities;
e) Through co-operation with partners.

My findings seem to suggest that the opportunities these companies successfully pursued combined external opportunity, internal opportunity (capability), and an ability to knit these all together.

In each company, effectiveness in developing an opportunity seemed to depend highly on the degree of interest and commitment the initiator received from top management. One critical aspect in this context seemed to be the ability to adequately describe the merits of the idea. At Dandy, the Russian opportunity was summarized using a simple formula, an "opportunity equation": Excess production capacity + Russian customers hungry for western products + cheap advertising + entrepreneurial Russian merchants = business opportunity.

At this stage in the business development process, opportunities remains in the mental realm, with initial discussions often leading to further considerations by the initiator, all of which is a process of refinement.

Refining opportunities

The refinement process initially involves thought on how action could be implemented in order to turn a given opportunity into reality. This can be difficult, because creating reality from opportunity often requires a company to do things that are completely new, and which thus involve uncertainty. Refinement also involves evaluation. I have observed that one critical skill is an ability is to do quick, rough calculations about the attractiveness of the opportunity. This seems to be much more important than thorough investigation. It is interesting to note that these companies appear to have focused on high-margin opportunities. Several believe you should try to make good profits quickly, because you never know how long the venture will last.

Predicting revenue from a new opportunity is recognized as involving great uncertainty. The case study companies therefore relied initially on instinctive judgment and improving the forecast as the venture unfolded. The important ability in determining revenue potential appears to have been an understanding of the critical driving force. For example, understanding the psychology of the new customers is highly valuable.

It seems to be true for many of the companies that they did not know, or indeed could not have known, from the outset just how big or attractive the opportunity would end up being. One of the areas included by these companies in this refinement process was ways of sharing risks (and rewards) to get projects off the ground.

Funding opportunities

Several of the case study companies emphasized the importance of getting projects off to a quick start, rather than allowing them to get bogged down in bureaucratic approval procedures. One of the companies spoke of an opportunity that was lost because business planning and the discussion of financial projections simply caused the project fade away.

In several of the companies, funding in the first stages of opportunity development was found within existing departmental budgets. Funding also seems to have been provided in small steps rather than in big ones. This makes it easier for an initiator to obtain funding for new investments. Agreement to big commitments up-front on uncertain ground can be difficult.

Implementing opportunities

The incremental learning approach was predominant in the companies studied. Learning by experimentation was often necessary because the opportunity was a new game with no established rules. One critical capability was the ability to develop a deep understanding of the opportunity environment, and to use that understanding to make the right strategic decisions. This is extremely difficult because the company may be operating at the limits of competence.

"Open" implementation in collaboration with customers is a favored model. The Politiken On Line service was developed in cooperation with its early users. One of them even wrote the user manual.

Timing and speed in implementation is essential, according to the case study companies. Opportunities must be capitalized on before they disappear, or before implementation becomes much more expensive. If Dandy had not reacted quickly in Russia, cheap advertising might not have been available, and the opportunity would have become less attractive.

Generally speaking, the case study companies seem to have developed their own rules for implementing projects. They did not rely on established procedures.

Managing the life-cycle of an opportunity

Several of the case study companies developed an understanding that different capabilities are needed at various stages in the life-cycle of an opportunity. The qualifications required during the start-up and introductory phases are not the same as those you need when an opportunity matures. At Dandy, for example, management of the Russian business opportunity was handed over after the final phase from one organizational unit to another.

Another characteristic of life-cycle management seems to be less control at the beginning of a venture, followed by tighter control as it matures. But throughout the life-cycle, an ability to learn first-hand from market reactions – from distributors, customers and competitors – and to adapt to them is critical to success. There are also political aspects to life-cycle management. Some opportunities, such as those linked to technology, have the potential ability to affect existing ways of working, and to influence power structures within an organization. Some of the companies studied said that a consistent "organizational massage" was needed as a consequence.

The importance of getting an opportunity off to a quick start has to be balanced by an ability to spot and kill dead-end opportunities. This seems to have been difficult for the case study companies, and it is an area to which any company embarking on opportunity-driven change should be alert.

Control

Monitoring opportunities is a tricky process because progress is often unpredictable and sometimes disappointing, compared with expectations. This is dangerous during the early life of an opportunity. The continuing faith of key sponsors seems to be critical to keeping an opportunity alive throughout difficult periods. Controlling new ventures by quickly isolating them into separate profit or cost centers was another approach preferred by some of these companies, all within the context of their desire to achieve short-term pay-back.

4.5 Organization and leadership

The organizational structure and principles differ considerably for each individual case study company. There are, interestingly, a number of organizational features that are in common, as well as individual characteristics.

An open and alert organization captures opportunities

I have observed that both "push" and "pull" measures are important in helping an organization generate and adapt to new opportunities. One company stressed the importance of keeping the organization alert and tuned to opportunity, and did so using continuous organizational development programs. Another company used a crisis as an excuse to push the organization into capitalizing on an opportunity. Yet a third company, Infogrames, favored creating an open organization where numerous partners have provided each other with sources of inspiration.

This last model is interesting because it provides a means of sharing financing, risks and rewards. It could be described as "interactive business development" (a particularly apt description in Infogrames' case) because the interactivity acts as a catalyst for the shaping of new business.

Politiken has used a reverse version of the Infogrames model, buying into opportunities and acquiring learning skills through joint- venture projects. In several of the companies, having a development partner or primary customer has often helped in obtaining initial project approval. However, the open-organization model makes project management and the ability to balance the interests of the various stake-holders highly critical.

Maintain the potential for funding initial exploration

One company argued that funding and time should always be found to explore new opportunities. This is important, since opportunities can often not be evaluated simply on the basis of an idea. Often the initial investment required to explore an opportunity is very small. Dandy's preliminary test advertising in Russia amounted to only $20,000.

Opportunity drive can be motivated by fun, "merchant skills" and teamwork, not by incentive schemes

Opportunity development can be driven by individuals both high and low in the organizational hierarchy. None of the companies studied has any special incentive scheme to motivate employees to develop opportunities. So what is the force behind opportunity development?

One source seems to be the satisfaction that can be derived from doing new things, creating the future. Another is what the Danes call *købmandskab,* which in a literal sense means simply "merchant skills", but the underlying meaning is "a nose for business". Several of the case companies valued a basic, hands-on merchant approach to business development. One company even tried to develop this as a part of its culture. For a "merchant" executive, business development is what makes the job fun. The attachment of value to merchant skills, we believe, supports several of the crucial factors needed for opportunity development, such as speed, quick calculation, making deals and the application of common sense to strategic decision-making.

Some of the companies favored employing and encouraging people who can think and act across functional borders, even though the company may look quite traditional (functional) on its organization chart. Opportunities are often born at the interface between different functional areas. One company underwent a job shuffle, in order to force production people to think in marketing terms, and vice versa.

Several opportunities were pursued by small teams released from bureaucratic control and given great personal freedom. The people working in these teams seemed to have great faith in their own ability, not necessarily to make the venture a success, but to explore it for the best obtainable outcome. Their belief in themselves also included the ability to learn from and live with disappointments. In all these companies, opportunities were furthered by fairly experienced people.

Visionary, hands-on leadership provides the right environment

I have found that, with the case companies, the ability to create a vision was critical. When insightful, the vision broadened thinking and stimulated employee opportunity drive. Hands-on management – rolling up their sleeves and getting their hands "dirty" – resulted in experiences that stimulated new business vision and the identification of new opportunities. It also acted as a foundation for a capacity to support opportunities spotted by others. In the companies studied, hands-on management included such activities as visiting new markets, listening to customer complaints first hand and testing new product concepts. At Politiken, one member of the top-management team even decided to change jobs to get directly involved in the development of a new business. In some of the smaller case companies, we found that top management was very instrumental in developing opportunities.

4.6 Conclusions

Strategic planning versus the opportunity approach

My findings suggest that, for a company facing radical industry or market change, strategic planning will probably not help promote a necessary change in direction. My own practical consulting experience supports this judgment on the shortcomings of the strategy discipline. Strategic planning may well be useful for the short-term optimization of a business, but when looking for new opportunities, whether or not this involves a change in direction, strategic planning is not the best tool for discovering them.

In the following chart, I have contrasted the two approaches to business development. In its most extreme form, strategic planning implies that everything not allowed for (in the plan) is forbidden. The opportunity approach implies that anything not forbidden is allowed. With the strategic planning approach, the strategy itself is the starting point, whereas with the business development approach, strategy is the end-result, a synthesis derived from experience.

The two contrasting approaches to business development

	Strategy approach	*Opportunity approach*
Catalyst	*yearly procedure*	*challenge logic*
Driver	*forms/manual*	*spirit*
Philosophy	*first think, then act*	*think and act*
Purpose	*make plan*	*develop opportunity*
Scope	*prepare big steps*	*think big, take smal steps*
Tools	*analysis*	*"merchant" capabilites*
Process	*sessions*	*field work*
Target	*goals/scorecards*	*opportunities/vision*
Direction	*plan*	*vision*

Focus activities in the opportunity approach

My findings suggest that an opportunity approach to business development should focus on:

- Challenging the existing business logic, to alert the company to new opportunities
- Stimulating opportunity seeking by using external catalysts (e.g. dissatisfied customers)
- Building new visions for specific business opportunities
- Refining and selecting the best opportunities
- Testing and evaluating the best opportunities by exploring them in the field
- Terminating unattractive opportunities and supporting attractive ones
- Synthesizing the emerging direction with lessons learned during the pursuit of opportunities.

Organizational hints

My findings also suggest a number of organizational hints for keeping the company opportunity-focused and capable of handling opportunities:

- Develop an open organization with many external links/partners;
- Train in "merchant" thinking (on/off job);
- Train in managing the opportunity-development life-cycle (on/off job);
- Provide the means for exchanging experience;
- Ensure that resources (time, money) are always available to explore opportunities.

The role of the external agent of change

Strategy is a discipline loved by consultants. But what role can they play in opportunity-based business development? In a typical strategy project, the division of responsibility between client and consultant is very clear: the consultant is responsible for strategic analysis and producing alternative strategies; the client decides on a strategy and implements it. If the challenge is to change strategic direction, however, the relationship is not so simple, because in such situations there is not much need for a packaged analysis, but rather for opportunity identification and development in the field.

There seem to be two obvious areas of opportunity-based business development to which consultants can add value:

1. *Preparation of an opportunity-focused organization.* This involves assisting the client company to become more open, to develop mechanisms for funding opportunities, to lower functional barriers against the exchange of acquired learning skills, and to provide training in opportunity development;
2. *Participation in opportunity discovery and development.* External consultants can stimulate opportunity discovery and participate in opportunity development in the same way that other external partners can, provided that they have the necessary competencies.

Involvement in the second area would represent a major change in the role of consultants. Participating in opportunity development means involvement in implementation, an area of strategy traditionally outside the realm of consultancy. It also means changing from working with a client to working within the client organization, perhaps even sharing the risk like other external partners.

Part Five

**Applying an opportunity-driven approach
to business development**

5.1 Introduction

In this chapter of the book, I shall propose specific ideas and concepts on how a company can quickly get started on exploring opportunities, and thus take the first steps towards changing direction. My views are based on the conclusions from all of the previous chapters as well as personal experiences from various consulting engagements. In order to motivate business people who read this book, I suggest practical hints and management techniques, my own and those of others, as well as further recommended reading.

My ideas are based upon two core beliefs. First, I believe that most companies possess a wealth of attractive opportunities. Most of these usually remain undiscovered, with only a few ever brought to attention, and in the best cases only one or two actually pursued. Second, I believe that many companies will soon find it necessary to employ an opportunity-driven and experimental approach to business development, especially in changing industries, simply because the future is so uncertain. (One of our case study companies explained this last point by stating that they could not plan any strategy for a new market that they or anybody else knew very little about.)

I have chosen to present ideas and suggestions in a systematized manner through the use of a model that recommends procedures for getting started on opportunity-based business development, and acquiring valuable knowledge in the process. The aim is to *kick-start* a process in which experimentation and learning may be the first steps towards a fundamental organizational transformation at a later stage. One of the most basic lessons to be learned from our case studies is thus applied to our own recommendations: *Begin with small steps, just as the case study companies took small steps in their opportunity pursuits, and gradually build understanding and commitment.*

This is an experimental model. Dan Muzyka of INSEAD has provided valuable comments. I aim to test it and, if necessary, to modify it on the basis of experience.

A process for opportunity-driven business development

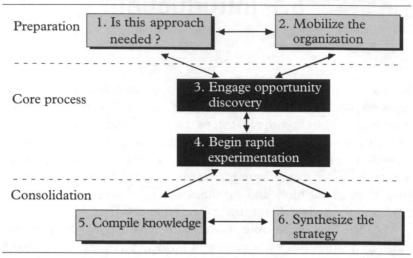

It needs to be emphasized that this model is not an attempt to reflect in any precise way the processes our case study companies have gone through. Rather, it is intended to highlight a sequence of activities that we suggest should be undertaken to obtain familiarity with the disciplines involved. The various arrows illustrate that many of the activities are interrelated, and that any subsequent application of the principles can be in an order other than what is suggested here – or even in an unstructured manner.

The principle of the model is very simple. First, I suggest that a quick common sense analysis be made to determine whether this approach is relevant, given a company's situation. Then I suggest various activities for mobilizing the organization to help people become more skillful in identifying and working with opportunities. Then comes the phase of opportunity discovery, followed by implementation-experimentation for the most attractive opportunities. The learning acquired from pursuing these opportunities needs to be collected and used for terminating opportunities, generating new ones, and gradually synthesizing the company's emerging strategy.

The goals of such a process should be:

• To create the means for stimulating both discovery of and experimentation with opportunities;

- To utilize learning as the basis on which a new direction for the company can gradually be formed;
- To demonstrate to an organization the value of opportunity pursuit that can change the fundamental thinking and logic of the company.

The model may give the impression that opportunity-driven business development is a linear process with a predictable outcome in the best rationalistic tradition. This is not the case. In practice, time spent on each phase will vary, and steps backwards will be taken. Rapid experimentation and learning, for example, may lead to new opportunity discoveries and provide input into how to mobilize an organization. It is also impossible to predict in the beginning just how large the opportunities may be.

Another warning: This is not a "one-size-fits-all" process. On the contrary, as suggested above, the first activity should be to diagnose the state of the business to judge whether this is what a company needs. If it is, any subsequent process should be tailored according to the findings of that diagnosis. I do, however, believe that this process could have been helpful to each of the companies studied before they changed direction, and could be useful to them today.

5.2 What approach does a company need?

Purpose

In the Wild West, there were traveling doctors who sold wonder medicines that, they claimed, could cure almost every disease. Of course, the products seldom delivered their promise. A parallel could be drawn between these wonder medicines and the wave of new management concepts that we have experienced during this post-war period, especially during the past 15 years. Some of these concepts have been marketed as wonder medicines, or have been applied by companies without much thought as to whether they were appropriate to that company's situation. Thus, the first stage should be to analyze whether the process I suggest is what your company really needs.

Suggestions

It would be a good idea for the company's management to spend a day, or even just half a day examining the following simple questions:

A. Where are we?
B. In which direction are we headed?
C. What do we need to do?
D. When do we need to do it?
E. What can trigger the process?

A. Where are we?

A SWOT analysis of a company's strengths, weaknesses, opportunities and threats is a good starting point for understanding both the situation and the needs of the organization. In this case, the concluding stage of the analysis should include the formulation of answers to numerous questions. Does the external environment, with its changes, require the company to change? Does the general performance of the company call for change? In connection with the latter question, understanding what the barriers are to opportunity drive and innovation is crucial. Are the elements blocking innovation related to culture, people, systems or structure? Money (or, rather, the lack of it) is seldom the sole answer!

A SWOT analysis is often a fairly subjective exercise. If, however, the process involves outsiders who know the company, this can help top management recognize the need to undertake a "change" project. Another way of increasing understanding of the company's situation is to analyze its life-cycle, for instance, by charting trends in turnover, profits and market share. It could be discovered that the company itself is a matured, stagnating company with little innovative ability.

B. Where are we headed?

A company will also need to determine what its current direction is and whether this is the right one in relation to the SWOT assessment. However, understanding a company's current direction cannot normally be achieved simply by reading the corporate business plan. It would be much more effective to consider projects currently being pursued, and to review any major decisions presently being made. From this, it could be determined whether any clear direction is even evident, or if there is indeed a need for a new direction.

C. What do we need to do?

One way of looking at this question in broad terms is to ask whether the company is generally doing the right things, but just needs to do them better (efficiency), or whether it needs to do new things (effectiveness). In the chart page 150, inspired by Muzyka et al. (1995), I indicate a number of approaches, with the choice depending upon the effectiveness and efficiency of the company:

The approach presented here primarily aims at increasing the effectiveness of a company through the pursuit of new business. I believe that these ideas can be valid even for very successful companies that are already both very efficient and very effective. Even with a healthy business, external change is a constant factor. Besides, it is

Management approaches to suit a company's situation

COMPANY EFFECTIVENESS

	Low	High
Low	Restructuring Transformation	Re-engineering
High	Opportunity approach Strategic planning	Business as usual Opportunity approach

COMPANY EFFICIENCY

often easier to obtain resource support for new opportunities when a company is doing well.

D. When do we need to do it?

It does not make much sense to pursue costly new opportunities if a company is undergoing a severe financial crisis. In some of the case study companies that had come through a crisis, I observed a two-step process. First came emergency cost-cutting and restructuring measures, and then the search for new opportunities. In management literature, use of the term "creative destruction" has become a popular way to describe long-term fundamental transformation that involves downsizing and simplifying, followed by regeneration of the organization and strategy.

The opportunity approach described in this report is, I believe, an alternative to the traditional process of renewing a business strategy. But when should it be preferred? The chart below suggests some indicators.

It is important to consider whether both fast results and the scale of change are needed. It should first be asked whether the company is faced with an evolutionary or radical change in its industrial sector. Initiating an opportunity-driven process for business development is in general not a problem quick fix, even though the ideas we have presented here have been for the purpose of getting the opportunity process started quickly.

Choosing between the strategy approach and the opportunity approach

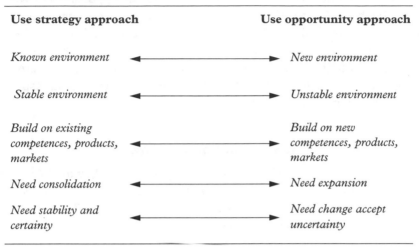

Use strategy approach	Use opportunity approach
Known environment	New environment
Stable environment	Unstable environment
Build on existing competences, products, markets	Build on new competences, products, markets
Need consolidation	Need expansion
Need stability and certainty	Need change accept uncertainty

The foundation of this process is an organization's capacity over time to learn from and build on its experiences in the pursuit of opportunities. Enacting such a process will certainly produce short-term gains in the form of learning. As was made evident from the experiences of the case study companies, it can also *produce business results fast.* Long-term gains, however, will depend on a company's ability to transform into a learning organization.

E. What triggers the process?

Doing the kind of analysis described above can be painful, but also eye-opening. It will hopefully lay a foundation for motivating senior management and other important stakeholders, in particular the company's owners and bankers to act according to the suggested management approaches. There is, however, a possibility that if this diagnostic process becomes too bureaucratic or painful, it could become a barrier to change rather than a cause of it.

Thus, this analysis is not without its drawbacks. Depending on the character and situation of the company concerned, it may prove beneficial to help senior management, owners and bankers understand and support the concept, particular if initiator(s) view them as potential sponsors. This can be accomplished by presenting a "package" that not only includes the results of the analytical process, but also illustrates the strength of the concept by using examples of how other companies have successfully pursued an opportunity-driven approach to change. Once it has been agreed that the opportunity-driven approach should be adopted, the process can introduced on anything from a small scale, such as by using business teams or divisions, to a large scale company-wide endeavor. Whichever route is chosen, the first step will be to mobilize the organization, an aspect considered in the next chapter.

Recommended reading

For this section I found ideas and concepts in the following:
Baden Fuller, C. and Stopford, J. M. (1992)
Muzyka, D., De Konning, A and Churchill, N. (1995)
Nolan, R and Croson, D. (1995)

5.3 Mobilizing an organization

Purpose

In our experience, strategy processes often neglect the mobilization of the entire organization. In a typical top-down strategy process, motivation is often limited to senior management selling a new strategy to other levels in the organization by using colorful booklets and pep talks, etc. Opportunity-driven change, however, is in large measure a result of the pursuit of opportunities by people at all levels in the company. It is this pursuit of opportunities at all organizational levels that creates the building blocks for the strategy finally synthesized by top management. Thus, mobilizing the organization is vitally important.

In this context, mobilizing an organization means encouraging people to *want to* pursue opportunities, allowing them the *capability* to do so, and providing the *means* and *conditions* necessary to make the process possible. This is a process that often demands fundamental changes in the way the company operates.

Mobilizing the organization

* Create a sense of urgency
* Enact new company rules
* Develop capabilites for handling opportunities
* Promote team work
* Empower employees
* Provide access to resources
* Strenghten the commitment of management
* Install evaluation and reward mechanisms

Suggestions

The art of mobilizing an organization for creativity, change and learning is the domain of organizational behavior experts and psychologists, and a topic that can be studied at great length. The suggestions outlined above, however, are not scientifically based. They are derived primarily from our observations of the practical methods used by the companies studied. I suggest the following eight focus areas:

Create a sense of urgency

Why should employees want to pursue opportunities? My cases have shown that employees who did so felt that trying new things was fun and interesting. Such enthusiasm may be a personal characteristic, but it can be transferred as a pull mechanism to other employees. More typical, perhaps, would be the push mechanism I have seen used, which is explaining the need to pursue opportunities in light of a company's situation. The future of a company may thereby be linked to the ability to capitalize on opportunities, creating a sense of urgency and commitment.

Enact new company rules

The successful pursuit of opportunity can be encouraged by explaining and acting in accordance with a set of "entrepreneurial game rules", such as:

- A failure is not a failure if we learn from it;
- Just do it;
- It is easier to be forgiven for something that you have done than to obtain permission for something you want to do;
- Be willing to take risks and we will reward you;
- Change jobs to get new ideas.

With active enforcement by management, such rules can over time become part of the company culture.

It is important to note that the same things that stimulate innovation do not necessarily stimulate effective implementation. Our case studies clearly demonstrate that opportunity projects should be managed loosely during the innovation phase, and more tightly in the later stages of implementation. Many elements that promote the generation of new ideas may demand tolerance of non-efficiency. The Danish company Oticon, for example, has installed a number of coffee bars in its headquarters, and encourages employees to take frequent "breaks" in order to stimulate cross-organizational communication.

Develop capabilities for handling opportunities

Some of the skills needed to handle opportunities can be acquired through training and ongoing on-the-job coaching. The following themes should be included in training programs:

Understanding and developing opportunity recognition

This includes an understanding of what an opportunity is, the phases of opportunity development (ending up with capturing the value and the psychological aspects of working with opportunities.

Strategic decision-making and the opportunity life-cycle

During the life-cycle of an opportunity, the team driving the opportunity will have to make a large number of strategic decisions, often under conditions of great uncertainty. Illustrating such decisions with cases can be helpful

Project management

One of the critical capabilities required for opportunity development is project control through disciplined management. The critical issue is not necessarily meeting targets, because this will often be difficult. Rather it is the ability to control the learning process on the basis of acquired experience.

Promote team work

Teamwork is a key element for both opportunity recognition and opportunity implementation. Effective teamwork requires great trust within the team and mutual recognition of each team member's worth. Appropriate reward for team efforts and results is also important. Peter Senge (1994) suggested that a new team could itself lay the foundations for effective collaboration by discussing the following questions:

1. Have you ever been part of a really great team?
2. What was different about that team?

3. How can we as a team create similar kinds of feelings here?
4. Which initiatives should we take to make our teamwork function?

During the early stages of developing an opportunity, a project may not involve full-time work for those involved. Others in the organization may therefore have to accept that some employees will have more than one job, and that team members work for two bosses.

Empower employees

Opportunity pursuit will be neither motivating nor effective if the team or individual employees are not empowered to make quick decisions when the need arises. My study clearly demonstrates that too much bureaucracy, such as application forms, project standards and approval procedures, can kill a project. The worst scenario is when such procedures kill a project slowly. Project-team members may experience a potentially long demoralizing fight with the bureaucracy, and in the end are forced to give up anyway. To aid in avoiding this, one simple way to provide freedom is to allocate a lump sum to a project and authorize the team to use it in any way they see fit, for example to test one or more of their ideas.

Provide access to resources

Opportunity recognition and development rely very much on access to resources such as knowledge and money. Some companies make information available throughout the organization by the use of sophisticated information systems. Another, very simple way to make people aware of knowledge that exists and where to find it is to encourage cross-functional, face-to-face communication. This can be promoted by various means, such as open office landscapes, relaxation areas and, more formally, presentations, workshops and brainstorming sessions (including electronic conferencing). Finally, of course, there is teamwork. Some companies, particularly those that are knowledge-intensive, even reward the active dissemination of knowledge, such as in personal performance reviews.

Regarding the allocation of money, we are not convinced that the establishment of an internal venture-capital department is the right way to fund opportunities. Simply keeping a degree of slack in budgets and raising external risk-sharing funds seems to have worked well for the case study companies. Allocating time is also a factor, since this is a critical resource necessary for exploring opportunities. The 3M method, allowing 15% of work time to be spent on personal projects, is one way of providing time for opportunity pursuit. In any event, for any company that is initiating opportunity pursuit as a "forced" activity, it will certainly be necessary to allocate time specifically to these endeavors.

Strengthen the commitment of management

Top management's role is crucial to opportunity pursuit. My study shows that the *attention, recognition* and *commitment* of management are major driving forces behind any opportunity team, especially during difficult times. Senior managers must, however, be careful not to develop such an affection for a given project that they begin to take it over, thereby running the risk of de-motivating its initiators. Top management has an important coaching role, especially as problem-solvers, throughout a project's life-cycle.

Install evaluation and reward mechanisms

None of my case study companies had specific reward mechanisms (e.g. financial incentives) for pursuing opportunities. I concluded that fun and curiosity were the major motivational forces. In my view, the proper reward mechanism is the opportunity for promotion. The establishment of a review committee is a good way to monitor the progress of opportunity pursuit, to acquire learning and to motivate teams.

Recommended reading

For this section, I found ideas and concepts in the following:
Peters, T. (1992)
Senge, P. et al (1994)
Block, Z. and MacMillan, I. C. (1993)

5.4 Engage in opportunity discovery

Purpose

 Opportunity discovery is at the heart of our process, the kick-start that leads directly to opportunity pursuit. This needs to be a natural element in any company's range of activities. The opportunity-discovery phase has three purposes:

- To search for opportunity ideas by scanning the environment as well as the internal resource base;
- To develop a portfolio of implementable opportunities;
- To evaluate and select opportunities for implementation experimentation.

Suggestions

I believe that this phase should include six activities:

The heart of the process – opportunity discoovery

1. Challenge the business logic

2. Define the opportunity space

3. Start the opportunity search

4. Refine opportunities

5. Develop an opportunity portfolio

6. Evaluate and select opportunities

1. Challenge the existing business logic

The purpose of the previous phase was to encourage motivation and curiosity. The phase I shall deal with now involves mentally challenging established ways of thinking in order to broaden the opportunity *horizon* and improve opportunity *alertness*. One of the most significant reasons for new ideas not being pursued is that they conflict with an existing business logic. We are, in a way, prisoners of our own experience. The more successful we are, the more difficult it is to challenge the existing business logic.

In his book, "The fifth discipline", Peter Senge (1990) included an effective illustration of business logic in the car industry. The American car industry's business logic until the 1960s included beliefs such as: a) our business is to make money, not cars; b) cars are primarily status symbols, so styling is more important than quality; c) the American car market is isolated from the rest of the world; and d) workers do not have an important impact on productivity or product quality. When new competitors from Germany and Japan began educating consumers about quality, it was difficult for the US industry to respond. In the process, foreign competitors increased their market share from nearly zero to 38% by 1986.

The inherent danger is that a company may not be aware of how its business logic guides its actions, and may thus be unable to locate the root cause for why decisions are ineffective. I believe that a company in this situation should first describe its existing logic, and then challenge it. One way of trying to uncover the existing business logic could be to begin by listing three recent major strategic moves the company has made, and three it decided not to make. Next, list the facts and beliefs these decisions were based on. The final stage of this exercise, finding the answers to why the company holds these beliefs and assumptions, should uncover the business logic. This process could identify perhaps five or ten basic assumptions, relating for instance to how to make money, how to manage, what the company does well and not so well. These assumptions will constitute the business logic.

Challenging a business logic can be facilitated by a series of "could" questions aimed at freeing participants from any existing logic by ignoring current constraints and imagining other possibilities:

- What other customers and needs could we serve?
- Could we make money in another way?
- Could we deliver benefits in another way?
- Could we be organized in a different way?

Another method is to identify and discuss trends that challenge an existing logic. Challenging your own norms can be very difficult, because you take them for granted. A way of avoiding this is to enlist the help of consultants, customers or colleagues not directly involved in this aspect of the company's business. An outsider's role is to ask basic questions, like, "Why do you do this?" and "Why do you do it in that way?". It is important for you to avoid defensive reasoning, and for any outsider to be completely honest and open.

One way of automatically refreshing a company's business logic could be to promote diversity in the organization, to ensure that those employed have a wide spectrum of profiles in terms of age, industry experience and company experience. As with biological organisms, an organization's long-term health depends in large measure on genetic variety.

2. Define the opportunity space

To maximize creativity in the opportunity search, it is important not to unduly influence those involved. Two forms of guidance are, however, important:

- Stating the ambition of the company to provide purpose for the opportunity search;
- Explaining the opportunity concept to provide a clue about what is being looked for.

A sense of purpose is important in generating emotional energy for the opportunity search. Top management must therefore link meaningful ambition to the activity. For example, in one company, the ambition was stated as follows: "We know that in 10 years our company should be completely different from what it is today. We want to start building the future now, and we want you to find some of the first stepping stones."

So just what is an opportunity? First of all, an idea itself might not necessarily be an opportunity, though opportunities are always driven by an original idea that, by the way, may undergo change during pursuit of the opportunity. Timmons (1990) defines an opportunity in the following way: "An opportunity is *attractive, durable* and *timely,* and is anchored in a product or service that *creates* or *adds value* for its buyer or end-user." Timmons (1990) also says that opportunities are often created in changing environments, chaos or inconsistencies – situations in which some see opportunities and others see nothing or see it too early or too late. This definition endows opportunity with a much bigger perspective than simply the development of a new product based upon a new technology.

My study shows that opportunities are often born from an ability to understand and combine elements, such as customer needs, technology, positioning and distribution. In this way, the company is able to see what others do not see. The opportunities relevant to the present discussion are those with the potential to generate new revenue – i.e. *not* internally focused opportunities, such as re-engineering initiatives with the aim of lowering costs. I am concerned here with effectiveness (doing the right things) not efficiency (doing things right).

The chart below provides an overview of opportunity space.

A definition of opportunity space

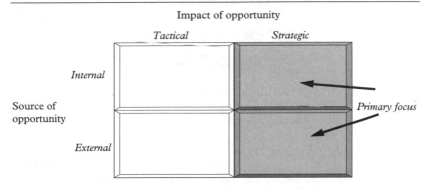

"Source of opportunity" refers to whether the opportunity originates internally, e.g. from exploiting competencies, or externally, e.g. from market changes. As we shall see later, opportunities usually arise as a match between external changes and internal competencies. The other dimension of the quadrant refers to the degree of impact on business. Some strategic opportunities are sought after because of their potential to radically change the way a company competes. Other such opportunities are pursued simply because they have the potential to generate a significant proportion (at least 20%) of company turnover in the long term. All other opportunities are considered tactical. In addition, there is yet another dimension to be kept in mind when defining opportunities, which I shall return to later, which is whether an opportunity is expected to produce economic value quickly or over time.

3. Start the opportunity search

In the chart below we present a possible way of organizing the opportunity search.

Organizing rapid opportunity search

Establish search guidelines – select search teams

Engage search teams

Discuss ideas

Identify opportunities

Refine opportunities

The principle of this search process is to begin by generating ideas, and then to combine and develop them into real opportunities. Here are a few basic guidelines which should assist in the search for creative ideas:

1. Set no limits;
2. Think beyond what we do today and how we do it – as if anything is possible;
3. Be naive and curious;
4. Ask "stupid" questions;
5. Take odd approaches and listen to odd people;
6. Try to see opportunities in threats.

Small teams can be formed, made up of three or four people who complement each other, who do not work together very often, and who have knowledge relevant to internal or external sources of opportunities. Each team could be given a specific opportunity-search area. They would then divide work into two phases, first exploring of the assigned area, followed by a brainstorming session to generate a list of opportunity ideas. This is, remember, still the idea stage. Proposals produced at this point are not necessarily implementable opportunities! Below I have listed possible search areas.

Focus areas of opportunity search

Functional	Cross-functional
• Customers	• Projects/abandoned projects
• Suppliers	• Unexpected events
• Partners	• Things that do not make sense
• Competitors	• Changes in perception
• Resources	• Trends
• Other industries	• The ideas of others
• Know-how institutions	

These areas will not be discussed further here. However, it should be noted that, as mentioned above, fuel for this exercise can also be generated by involving external agents. Forming a team for each area means that the exercise will have many participants, which is precisely the idea. The use of employee suggestion boxes can expand the number even more.

Once each search team has produced a list of opportunity ideas, this wealth of ideas should be brought together to begin the process of combining them into one or more potentially plausible opportunities. There thus needs to be some form of inter-team review process involving presentation and discussion.

4. Refine opportunities

Each original team, or perhaps reorganized teams, should now be given the task of refining any potentially viable opportunities. This process would involve crafting and visualizing. Each team should concentrate on one opportunity. Crafting and visualizing is a very important step that is frequently not undertaken. Companies may well have ideas, but few convert them into genuine opportunities. My study has shown how important it is to be able to envision the implementation of an opportunity.

Crafting is the process of combining often internal and external elements into a logical concept.

Visualizing is making an opportunity come alive by answering questions such as:

- Why should we pursue the opportunity?
- What can we achieve (vision)?
- What does the value proposition look like to us and to the customer (economic benefits)?
- What are the success factors?
- What should we do to begin implementation?

The result of this refinement exercise should be a proposal (using text, graphics, drawings, or whatever best captures the essence of the opportunity) which is then presented to the other teams.

5. Develop an opportunity portfolio

Some of the executives in the companies studied told us that it was often difficult for them to achieve an overview of all company opportunities/ideas. And they often asked themselves whether the right ones were being pursued. The management team can, we suggest, establish such an overview by developing an opportunity portfolio, from which opportunities can be reviewed allowing a broader company perspective. Below is a model for such a portfolio.

As can be seen, the model operates using four different types of opportunities, categorized according to their potential impact (tactical or strategic) and their nature (immediate or emerging). Typical new ventures or business start-ups can often be characterized as targeting available opportunities that differentiate the business from

The opportunity portfolio

Impact of opportunity

	Tactical	Strategic
Immediate	Easy pick	Typical new venture
Emerging	?	Learning opportunity

Nature of opportunity

those of companies already on the market. When changing strategic direction, companies must also work with another category that is less obvious, and that is learning opportunities. An example of such an opportunity could be a newspaper experimenting with on-line media, not knowing the business potential of doing this but sensing enormous strategic potential in the new technology.

The opportunities that any given company should focus on depend on the situation of the company, as diagnosed in the first phase. It is obvious that the number of projects a company can pursue at any given time will be limited, though the need for new direction could be a reason for starting up more new projects, while terminating others. Balancing the portfolio means pursuing projects with "big win", long term potential, as well as projects in which value can be capitalized on in the shorter term.

6. Evaluate and select opportunities

A quick evaluation of each opportunity naturally should be made by management before selecting any for the experimentation phase. The following set of questions, inspired by Dan Muzyka of IN-SEAD, could be used to help establish criteria for selection:

Scale: Does the opportunity have enough potential to satisfy ourselves as well as our stakeholders?

Scope: Is there sufficient value added (gross margin and learning) in the opportunity, and can it lead to new opportunities?

Window: Can we exploit the opportunity long enough to capitalize
            on the value and what is learned?

Risk: Does the potential benefit from the opportunity match the
            risks?

One evaluation criterion that clearly should *not* be used is whether
the opportunity fits with the existing direction of the company. I rec-
ommend usage of the "quick but with common-sense" evaluation
that I saw used by the case study companies. The opportunities selected should be considered experiments, since each involves tre-
mendous uncertainty, rather than as fully developed venture
projects. It is therefore preferable to start up many such project, and
to kill many as well. This philosophy is also supported by the fact innovation is, to some degree, a numbers game. The more experiments made, the more likely it is that success will be achieved.

In small and medium-sized companies, the lack of qualitative or
quantitative resources is often mentioned as a reason for decisions
not to pursue opportunities. My casework suggests a few ways of
getting further mileage out of limited resources:

Creating or utilizing networks. By entering into joint ventures or alliances with other companies, it may be possible to obtain access to
knowledge or capabilities. You might discover skills you were previ-
ously unaware that already existed internally or among your closest
partners, such as suppliers and distributors. One way to detect these
is by making personal capability profiles.

Obtaining quick pay-back. Some of our case study companies focused intensively on obtaining positive cash flow and pay-back within a short space of time. This helps generate resources for other opportunities.

Re-use what you have. When resources are scarce, re-using those
you have can be a good idea. This can, for example, include re-using
brands, re-using information or repackaging products for a different
segment.

Seeing several opportunities in one. An opportunity is not just an opportunity. Some of those pursued by the companies studied included additional sources of value. For example, providing a medium
which generated revenue from both subscribers and advertisers. Al-
ternatively, an initial opportunity may lead to a stream of new opportunities.

Opportunities not selected for further pursuit should not be altogether scrapped, but visibly "banked" to provide inspiration, and to be available if the right moment ever arrives.

Recommended reading

For this section I found ideas and concepts in the following:

Senge, P. (1990)
Timmons, J. (1990)
Drucker, P. (1985)
Grant, R., (1994)
Hamel, G. and Prahalad, C.K. (1994)

5.5 Begin rapid experimentation

Purpose

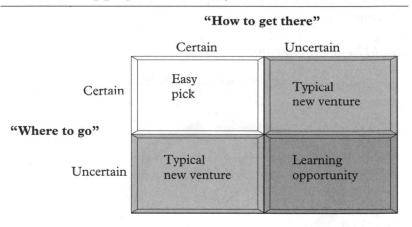 I have deliberately called this phase "rapid experimenta-
tion" instead of "rapid implementation", because the latter
indicates projects in which it is known where to go and how
to get there. In opportunity-driven change, the vision of where to go
can be blurry, as can "how to get there". Such projects demand experimentation. The chart below makes the point using a diagram:

Characterizing project uncertainty

"How to get there"

	Certain	Uncertain
Certain	Easy pick	Typical new venture
Uncertain	Typical new venture	Learning opportunity

"Where to go" (applies to the Certain / Uncertain rows)

I have included in this matrix the different types of opportunity we
defined earlier. The easy pick is often straightforward, but may have
limited potential. Typical new ventures often involve some degree of
uncertainty. If not, they would be too obvious and thus probably not
particularly attractive. Learning opportunities are normally the most
difficult and uncertain. Thus, bearing this matrix in mind when
dealing with opportunity projects will help you treat them differently
from "easy picks", especially in terms of support and follow-up.

Suggestions

1. Organizing the projects

I believe it to be of fundamental importance to have those people who identified the opportunity, and are thus very committed to it, given a role in the start-up. As my cases show, however, there are different approaches to organizing opportunity projects: creating a separate project group, turning the activity over to a line function, or having the CEO as its champion. Several of the companies studied, once the opportunity/project had reached a certain size, were keen to organize the project under a business unit/division, with some kind of bottom-line responsibility.

2. A method for rapid experimentation

Experimentation should be based on common sense, where a given action is taken, learning ensues, and new action follows based on the experience. The model in this diagram is a framework for rapid experimentation.

Rapid experimentation

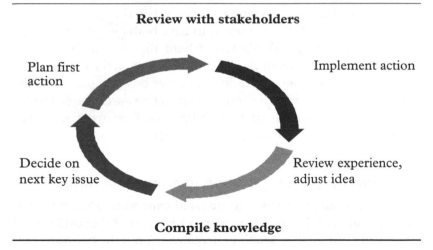

Review with stakeholders

Plan first action

Implement action

Decide on next key issue

Review experience, adjust idea

Compile knowledge

The starting point for experimentation is to *plan the first actionable step*. My case study companies stressed the importance of not suffocating opportunities by subjecting them to bureaucratic approval procedures and planning demands. In my view, it is not fruitful to begin opportunity experimentation by drafting a business plan. This is, in any event, impossible in any meaningful sense when a project leads into the unknown.

Nevertheless, healthy thinking about how to get started is useful. The process could begin with a brainstorming session, listing potential experimentation activities. For example, the team could write a short paper (four or five pages) outlining the results of an opportunity-visualization exercise, any proposed initial action, and the resources required. The purpose in all this is to gain experience necessary to support the validity of the opportunity. I am not thinking here of desk-based market research, but of real-life experimentation, such as rapid prototype development or market experimentation.

During and after implementation of the first step, the team must *review the experience* in relation to a) any project assumptions (which may well lead to adjustment of the idea), b) where to go with it, and c) the potential next steps. The team should then decide what the next major step will be, and start planning the activities involved. And so the cycle continues.

It is important to recognize that the original idea seldom remains the one that is successfully implemented. It often has to be modified, though this might be difficult for its originator(s) to accept, which is one of the reasons why external review is important.

I believe it to be useful for teams to have both *formal and informal review meetings* with stakeholders, where the idea itself and the progress in achieving it are challenged. Based upon the case studies, I also believe teams should produce a proper business plan once the project has matured and the commitment of resources begins to increase. The compilation of knowledge based on what has been learned will be considered in the next section.

Success factors relating to experimentation

What are the success factors in the rapid experimentation phase? A study on successful ventures by Muzyka et al. (1987) provides food for thought. As well as looking at issues relating to business concepts, the study highlights the importance of good management. A poor concept can sometimes be rescued by good management, but a good concept will not rescue poor management. The study identities four success factors relating to venture management that we find particularly interesting:

- a proven, integrated management team;
- experience in start-up management and industry;
- ability to maintain focus on key success factors;
- appropriate general management and employee incentives.

I have already mentioned the resistance to change that often dogs new opportunities. This is understandable, given that successful exploitation of new opportunities, especially technology-related ones, may well destroy existing ways of doing business. The ways in which new technology has changed and will continue to change the newspaper business is an obvious example. Management skill in handling resistance to change is therefore critical. Equally, top management must be able to differentiate between managing mature businesses, and those that are emerging.

Recommended reading

For this section, I found concepts and ideas in the following:

Muzyka, D, Timmons J., Stevenson H., Bygrave, W. (1987)

5.6 Compile knowledge

Purpose

The purpose of this phase is to digest the fundamental – i.e. strategic – knowledge acquired during the pursuit of an opportunity. We thus suggest a compilation of what has been learned. Opportunity teams should acquire a fair amount of knowledge during project implementation. Thus, fundamental knowledge, based upon what has been learned, can be exchanged and documented at review meetings.

Suggestions

Profiting from experience is very much a question of being open and willing to learn, even from what some people might consider to be a failure. Generally, people have a narrow and negative understanding of the meaning of failure, and therefore tend to hide from it, a reflex that can block valuable learning. What may seem to be a failure can actually lead to new opportunities, especially if the knowledge acquired from the failed project can be exploited. Below are a number of questions that can serve as a starting point for the assimilation of learning

How to ask learning questions

1. What went well and why?
2. What went less well and why?
3. What would we do differently now?
4. What would we do the same way?

5. What went unexpectedly well and why?
6. What went unexpectedly badly and why?

7. Are there new assumptions/rules to be made?

8. Why did we not foresee what happened?
9. How can we improve learning in the future?

Source: T. Grundy (1994) p. 15

Learning questions should focus on both project content and the project-development process. The trick is to generate double-loop learning: to learn what works and what does not, and about the assumptions (business logic) that lie behind why it works or why it does not. During reviews, it is important not only to digest what is learned, but also either to renew the commitment and motivation necessary to keep the project going, or to terminate it.

Recommended reading

For this section, I found ideas and concepts in the following:

Argyris, C. (1991)
Grundy, T. (1994)

5.7 Synthesize the strategy

Purpose

A new strategic direction seldom *emerges*. A large amount of active brainwork is usually needed. Focusing on a new direction, not blindly following it, serves two purposes. First, it helps promote a realignment of resources, both now and in the future, that can make the company more competitive. Second, more specifically, it provides guidelines for allocating resources to competencies and capabilities, the roots of a company's future business.

The knowledge acquired in the previous phase will assist in narrowing the company focus of direction. If a company is in a turbulent environment, or if it thrives on a relatively unstructured way of operating, this phase should not be thought of as the first step towards a detailed top-down restatement of the strategic focus for everyone in the company. Rather, the purpose of this phase is to create a sense of direction and to narrow the window of opportunity.

Suggestions

What is strategy synthesis? The Encyclopedia Britannica defines synthesis as: "...in philosophy, the combination of parts or elements in order to form a more complete view or system. The coherent whole that results is considered to show the truth more completely than a mere collocation of parts".

Another way to understand synthesis is to compare it to analysis. In strategic planning, analysis is often used to split a question into smaller parts. For example, the question, "Can market share be increased?", can be broken down into, "Can we meet the needs of our customers in a better way?", and, "Can we increase share by changing prices?". These questions can then be split into sub-questions. Synthesis is the reverse process. It is a means of seeing an overall vision or direction on the basis of a number of elements, looking particularly at what the company does well, and lessons learned from experience. The diagram below illustrates the difference.

Synthesizing vision is a natural job for top management, since developing an overview, a broad understanding of what is going on in the company, is a managerial responsibility. Synthesizing strategy, however, is a gradual process of clarification that may involve a wider spectrum of employees. The illustration below outlines the strategy synthesis process.

The difference between analysis and synthesis

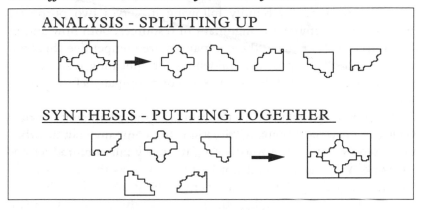

ANALYSIS - SPLITTING UP

SYNTHESIS - PUTTING TOGETHER

In some of the companies studied, it took years for a new direction to crystallize. The process takes time because it is based on an assortment of strategic decisions, experiences, results and new business logic that are acquired during the pursuit of an opportunity.

The following elements should be included in the synthesis process.

1. Fundamental beliefs

The new direction should build on a set of fundamental beliefs, including:

- business logic
- new discoveries, including what a company does well
- a view of the future
- major areas of opportunity.

Synthesizing strategy

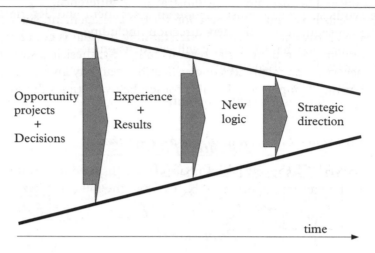

The depth of understanding supporting these fundamental beliefs is critical. I observed in one of the case study companies that a direction/strategy built on powerful insights was highly motivating and trustworthy.

2. Umbrella vision

An umbrella vision provides a broad sense of direction. Based on the fundamental beliefs, it should include corporate *aspirations*, a logical *idea* of the business that can be easily understood, and a *purpose*. This combination will provide a sense of business scope and the types of needs the company wishes to satisfy. The level of detail will depend on the level of uncertainty in the assumptions.

Whether or not the direction should be accompanied by specific quantitative or qualitative goals depends on whether the company believes such goals to be helpful from a managerial and/or motivational point of view. Our findings from the casework suggest that such goals are not needed. The new direction must be one that engages the emotional energy of employees. It should thus be broadly communicated and discussed.

3. Consequences

The synthesis process must include an assessment and description
of the consequences of the new direction, including:
- decisions on what a company will *not* focus on
- activities it will discontinue
- key challenges
- he focus for business development.

Potential pitfalls

Strategy synthesis involves potential pitfalls. Inspired by Mintzberg
(1994), I believe it important to be aware of the following hazards:

1. Premature change

When decisions are made about a change in direction, there is always the risk of making the change too quickly, either because of im-
patience, or because of a desire to reduce uncertainty in the organization.

2. The "soul" of an idea can be lost

It can be difficult to adequately express an idea on paper. The spirit
or force of the strategy may be diluted. This may not be an issue for
those who came up with the strategy, but it could become a big
problem when it has to be communicated to others. This is why
face-to-face communication about the new strategy is so important.
Use of metaphors or analogies also help bring it to life. One of our
case study companies (an entertainment software company) explained its vision using analogies from the film and TV industry.

3. Experimental drive slows down

As the direction to be taken becomes clearer and preparatory work
more structured, the organization tends to become more focused. In
turn, this may lead to a "cooling off" of the experimental drive.
However, if a company is in a turbulent environment, the making of
a decision to go in a new direction should not in itself be allowed to
limit the organization's sensitivity to its external environment. They

should continue to allow for the potential need for further adjustment.

4. Too much attention to numbers

Many companies focus on the establishment of higher quantitative goals for turnover and earnings. A company's financial objectives are, however, not a strong motivational force for employees, unless their remuneration is heavily influenced by success or failure in reaching these goals. It is therefore important to have a deeper purpose: What would the world lack if the company did not exist? That is to say, what is the basic value that the company provides?

Incorporating opportunity driven business development

The circle will be completed when a company once again compares its direction with the overall corporate situation- the first step of the opportunity driven business development process. Having gone through the opportunity process a company is in the process of learning how to handle opportunities and is on its way to developing organizational and human capabilities and principles for this. *However, the next challenge will not necessarily be to go through the same process and sequence of activities once again, because that process will only have been intended to kick-start opportunity-based business development. The next step will be to utilize the methods and principles the company found valuable.*

Recommended reading

For this section I found ideas and concepts in the following:

Mintzberg, H., *The rise and fall of strategic planning*, Prentice Hall 1994

Part Six

Final remarks

6.1 The main points in this book

This book is by no means an exhaustive investigation into opportunity-driven business development. Rather, it should be seen as a first step along the road, based upon what I have learned from my casework, my own ideas, and inspiration derived from various experts in Entrepreneurship, corporate venturing, organizational behavior and other disciplines. The experimental approach I propose for business development resembles the activities of some companies in the area of product development. As one company executive put it: "An experimental approach to business development could draw from experiences in experimental, no-limits product development. But when it is about business development, much more is at stake for the company and the persons in charge."

Some use a greenhouse metaphor to help understand experimental product development. However, I do not believe that this metaphor is relevant to opportunity-based business development. Pursuing opportunities has little to do with a "safe" greenhouse. It is more like a chaotic chemical reaction. I have frequently emphasized the differences between strategic-planning and an opportunity-based approach. The differences can perhaps be most clearly explained by listing some of the problems linked to strategic planning, and contrasting them to opportunity-driven change.

1. Strategic planning provides few new ideas

Opportunity-driven change focuses on new ideas. Even more important, it involves experimentation with selected opportunities.

2. Strategic planning involves so much analysis and planning that it affects resources and mental energy that could be put into implementation

Opportunity-driven change begins with implementation (or, rather, experimentation) and ends with the definition of a strategic direction based upon what has been learned.

3. Strategic planning produces paper rather than direct business value

The aim of opportunity-driven change is to create value from opportunities, right from the very beginning.

4. Strategic planning often ends up with a consensus strategy rather than a change in direction

Opportunity-driven change is based on taking small steps, letting the results and knowledge obtained from those steps provide sound business arguments for change. Our cases have shown that it is easier to get $100,000 for an experiment in a new market than to get $1m to develop a new market.

5. Strategic planning is infected by a language problem, which is that everybody is uncertain about the definition of core concepts such as vision, mission, goals and strategy

The aim of the opportunity-driven approach is not to talk in management language, but the language of the business opportunities that are being pursued.

6. Strategic planning is a top-down process that takes little or no account of new ideas in an organization

With opportunity-driven change, the process begins with the mobilization of the entire organization in order to discover and formulate opportunities.

6.2 A Summary in ten main points

I believe that 10 main points can be derived from our research in this area:

1: Changes in strategic direction come from the pursuit of opportunities rather than from strategic planning.
2: Opportunity drive is motivated by vision, curiosity and a nose for business, rather than by goal-setting. It is also motivated by providing an organization with the capabilities for opportunity pursuit, rather than by fancy pep talks.
3: The discovery of new opportunities is often triggered by contradictions and chaos, rather than by logic or order.
4: Companies should embark not only on typical (safe) ventures, but also on uncertain (learning) ventures.
5: Strategies do not simply emerge, they need to be synthesized from experience, insight and foresight.
6: "Opportunity space" should not be delineated by existing products, markets or even competencies, but rather by what an organization believes to be future opportunities.
7: Companies should be able to stimulate and control both existing, mature businesses and new opportunities. The strategic-planning approach is primarily relevant to the former, whereas the opportunity-driven approach applies more to the second category. However, as opportunity-driven business development projects mature, strategic planning will begin to have increasing relevance.
8: Even companies that currently do not consider themselves to be innovative or entrepreneurial are able to kick-start a process of opportunity-driven business development and learn to become innovative and entrepreneurial.
9: Pursuing opportunities often requires the "destruction" of existing business activities or ways of doing business. This can lead to resistance to new opportunities, a problem that needs to be addressed at the beginning of the process.
10: Carpe diem (or in plain English: Pursue your opportunities!)

References

Argyris, C.: *Teaching smart people how to learn,* Harvard Business Review May-June 1991

Baden Fuller, C. and Stopford, J. M.: *Rejuvenating the mature business,* Routledge 1992

Bhide, Amar: *How Entrepreneurs Craft Strategies That Work,* Harvard Business Review, March-April 1994

Block, Z. and MacMillan, I. C.: *Corporate venturing,* Harvard Business School Press 1993

Churchill, N.: *Starting Down The Information Highway,* INSEAD case 1995

D'Aveni, R: *Hypercompetition,* The Free Press 1994

Drucker, P.: *Innovation and Entrepreneurship,* Heinemann 1985

Economist Intelligence Unit: *The Automotive Industry*

Ernst & Young (1994); *Biotech 95*

Ghoshal, S.: *Competing On Capabilities,* Canon, INSEAD case 1992

Grant, R.: *Contemporary strategy analysis,* Blackwell 1994

Grundy, T.: *Strategic learning in action,* McGraw-Hill 1994

Hamel, G. & Prahalad, C.K.: *Competing For The Future,* Harvard Business School Press 1994

Hamel, G. & Prahalad, C.K: *Strategic Intent,* Harvard Business Review, May-June 1989

Kotter, J.: *What Leaders Really Do,* Harvard Business Review, May-June 1990

Mintzberg, H.: *The rise and fall of strategic planning,* Prentice Hall 1994

Muzyka, D., De Konning, A and Churchill, N.: *On adaptation and transformation: building the entrepreneurial corporation,* European management journal, December 1995

Muzyka, D, Timmons J., Stevenson H., Bygrave, W.: *Opportunity recognition: the core of Entrepreneurship,* Frontiers of Entrepreneurship Research 1987

Nevens T., Summe, G. & Uttal, B.; *Commercializing Technology: What The Best Companies Do,* Harvard Business Review, May-June 1990

Nolan, R and Croson, D.: *Creative destruction*, Harvard Business School Press 1995

Peters, T.: *Liberation management*, McMillan 1992 (rather, flip through it)

Senge, P.: *The fifth discipline*, Doubleday 1990

Senge, P. et al: *The fifth discipline field book*, Doubleday 1994

Smith, R.: *The Global Car Market*, Purchasing and Supply Management, June 1994

Strebel, P.: *Breakpoints*, Harvard Business School Press 1992

Timmons, J.: *New venture creation*, Irwin 1990

Treacy M., Wiersema F.: *The discipline of the market leaders*, Harper Collins 1995

United Nations: *World Investment Report 1994*